A Man
ARMCHAIR

FBI

MYTHS AND MISCONCEPTIONS

DEBUNKING CLICHES FOR THOSE WHO READ,
WATCH, AND WRITE CRIME DRAMAS ABOUT
THE FBI OR HAVE ALWAYS WANTED TO BE A
SPECIAL AGENT

JERRI WILLIAMS

FBI Myths and Misconceptions: A Manual for Armchair Detectives

Cover design by Teddi Black
Interior design by Megan McCullough

This FBI manual is dedicated to my parents, Buford and Odessa Williams.

I'm blessed to have grown up in a loving home where books were valued, and reading was encouraged.

"If the art of the detective began and ended in reasoning from an armchair, my brother would be the greatest criminal agent that ever lived."

—Sherlock Holmes

(Sir Arthur Conan Doyle - *The Greek Interpreter*)

CONTENTS

THE MISSION

Public Perception of the FBI

I'm a retired FBI agent reliving my glory days writing crime fiction about greed and corruption and hosting *FBI Retired Case File Review*, a true crime and history podcast featuring interviews with other retired special agents. I'm on a mission to show the public who the FBI is and what the FBI does through my books, my blog, and my podcast case reviews with former colleagues.

Most people have never met an FBI agent in person. What they know about the FBI comes from popular culture, their only connections being those made by reading books and watching TV shows and movies about the Bureau. Of course, there's also what they have heard and seen from the news media. Is that you? Well… what if the things you've been reading and watching were stuffed with clichés and misconceptions?

Do you know who the FBI is? Do you know what the FBI does?

Depending on your generation, your early knowledge of the FBI might have come from watching Jimmy Stewart in the 1959 movie, *The FBI Story*. Baby boomers also remember well *The F.B.I.*, the television series starring Efrem Zimbalist Jr. It was one of the most popular shows on TV from 1965 to 1974. Today, the public continues to be intrigued with the FBI, reflected in an attention-grabbing collection of bestselling novels, major box office hits, and popular TV shows, all powerful promotional tools, practically commercials, for the FBI. These entertaining films and fiction are also recruiting tools for those who might want to join the FBI. Television viewers recently enjoyed a reboot of the cult classic *X-Files* where agents Fox Mulder and Dana Scully investigated paranormal phenomena. Shows like the *X-Files* heighten curiosity about the FBI. Throughout *FBI Myths and Misconceptions: A Manual for Armchair Detectives* I'll introduce you to a number of successful portrayals of the FBI, and others that are not so successful.

I've always been a reader and a storyteller, and after serving twenty-six years as a special agent in the FBI, I have plenty of stories to tell. During most of my Bureau career, I worked major economic fraud investigations and was amazed at the schemes con artists and corrupt corporate and public officials would devise to steal other people's money. I was fortunate to have been assigned several complex advance-fee, Ponzi scheme, and business-to-business telemarketing cases and to have received numerous awards throughout my career, including four United States Attorney Awards for Distinguished Service. I've also had the opportunity to work bank robberies and drug investigations. The one thing I know for sure is: "With a gun, you can steal hundreds. With a pen, you can steal millions."

Nearing the end of a successful career specializing in cases targeting fraud and corruption, I was appointed to serve as the media representative and spokesperson for the Philadelphia Division during my last five years. In that role, I was responsible for educating and informing the media and the public about the FBI, in an effort to mold and massage people's perception of the FBI. That meant I was often out in front of local and national news media. I also was tasked with answering questions about the FBI when asked by crime writers like the Philadelphia-based, best-selling author Lisa Scottoline. I worked with producers and directors from the History Channel, *America's Most Wanted*, the Discovery Channel, and big-budget films on their FBI-focused projects, and I appeared on the long-running CNBC show *American Greed* when one of my Ponzi scheme cases was featured on the show. After I retired from the FBI in 2008, I was hired for a high-profile corporate position in media relations and public affairs and learned even more about the value of public perception.

I'm telling you all of this to explain why I care so much that the FBI be portrayed accurately and fairly and how I'm uniquely experienced to take on this mission to show the public who the FBI is and what the FBI does.

Fortunately, while producing and hosting my podcast *FBI Retired Case File Review* I've been able to directly introduce the public to former FBI agents. The episodes provide a behind-the-scenes look at some of the FBI's most famous cases, along with many not-as-well-known investigations. I believe it's important to satisfy the public's curiosity about the Federal Bureau of Investigation by showing the human side of special agents and how they handle the challenges of working for the Bureau. During almost every interview, one of us comments about some aspect of the case or an investigative method that had been inaccurately portrayed in books, TV, and movies or as a cliché. Over time, I've noted numerous misconceptions about the FBI that we repeatedly discussed.

My colleagues and I have found these falsely drawn portrayals annoying and frustrating. Just as some attorneys don't read or watch legal dramas and some doctors avoid medical shows and novels, there's a good chance some FBI agents aren't reading that bestselling book series or watching that popular show depicting the FBI. They can be difficult to engage in without hurling the book across the room or wanting to throw a shoe at the TV.

I gave a presentation to the New York Chapter of the Mystery Writers of America (MWA) regarding my original ten myths and also noted them in *FBI Retired Case File Review* episode 50. In episode 100, I increased the number from ten to twenty and presented the expanded FBI reality checklist during presentations to the Delaware Valley Chapter and the Atlanta Chapter of Sisters in Crime. My well-received speech and the anniversary podcast episodes are the inspiration and foundation for *FBI Myths and Misconceptions: A Manual for Armchair Detectives*.

FBI Facts vs. Fiction

Why should we care if entertainment media gets things wrong about the FBI in books, TV, and movies? First of all, an educated audience is mentally thrown out of a story each time they read or watch something that's inaccurate about the FBI. That's not good. I'm sure writers want to keep readers and viewers engaged. Second of all, when someone writing a novel, script, or screenplay gets essential facts wrong and falsely portrays FBI procedures and personnel, hundreds of thousands, possibly millions, of people now believe erroneous information about the FBI. It makes more sense to break the rules after you've learn what the rules are.

If fictional FBI agent characters are relegated to investigating only one or two types of violation(s) or if they are written in negative and unflattering ways, when real FBI agents call someone on the phone or show up at a business or home to investigate actual cases, the response and cooperation they receive will, no doubt, be influenced by the last book that person read or TV show they watched about the FBI. And inaccuracies in film and fiction could have life-changing consequences for someone accused of a federal crime and on trial. Based solely on the depiction of trials and how agents testify on TV, members of the jury may have expectations about what they see and hear in court and the investigative actions of FBI agents. It's not difficult to understand how their vote for or against a guilty verdict could be influenced by preconceived notions, instead of the facts presented.

I'm aware that many of the clichés and misconceptions presented in *FBI Myths and Misconceptions: A Manual for Armchair Detectives* are intentionally written into books, scripts, and screenplays due to time constraints and the need to create well-paced scenes and fully developed characters. These shortcuts are needed, at times, to tell a story in an entertaining way. Retired FBI agent Bobby Chacon, my co-host for *FBI Retired Case File Review* episode 50 and episode 100, works as a writer and technical adviser for television and film. He calls those intentional errors "creative compromises." This is especially true for TV shows. During the creative process, it is understood and accepted that in a one-hour drama (forty-two minutes to be exact, taking into account commercials), showrunners must quickly move the story from beginning to end. Attempting to create an accurate portrayal of an FBI investigation is an almost impossible task when the investigation must be solved in less than an hour. FBI agents must accept that when authors are crafting their novels or writers are drafting a script for a prime-time TV show or feature film, they are writing for a general audience. They are not writing for the professional law enforcement officer or FBI agent. The truth is that most readers and viewers simply want to be entertained, and they are not all that concerned about accuracy or being educated. Facts are simply things that don't always move the action forward.

I mentioned earlier that most readers and viewers have never met a real agent, but it should also be noted that most scriptwriters have never met an FBI agent either. Bobby Chacon told me that on many of the shows he has worked on, he is the first FBI agent that those preparing the script have met. I must assume that the majority of the authors of thrillers, crime novels and mysteries with FBI characters are writing their stories based on what they learned about the FBI from other books, TV shows, and films. That would account for the common clichés and misconceptions that are being repeated again and again.

From the FBI Website

"Frequently Asked Questions"
How accurately is the FBI portrayed in books, television shows, and motion pictures?

Any author, television scriptwriter, or producer may consult with the FBI about closed cases or our operations, services, or history. However, there is no requirement that they do so, and the FBI does not edit or approve their work. Some authors, television programs, or motion picture producers offer reasonably accurate presentations of our responsibilities, investigations, and procedures in their storylines, while others present their own interpretations or introduce fictional events, persons, or places for dramatic effect.

(https://www.fbi.gov/about/faqs/how-accurately-is-the-fbi-portrayed-in-books-television-shows-and-motion-pictures)

The most important thing for the writer is the story. That means that those creative compromises mentioned earlier will, most likely, need to be made in order to tell a good tale. First, the storyline and characters are created, and then the details are layered on. Facts are added last to complete and deepen the plot. But the story must always come first.

For armchair detectives who do want to learn about the real FBI, in *FBI Myths and Misconceptions: A Manual for Armchair Detectives* I'll provide a reality check. My reality checks should not be confused with criticism. As I previously acknowledged, due to time constraints sometimes corners must be cut, and creative license must be used to move matters along quickly. I get it. I really do. But to counteract the "CSI effect"—a term that refers to the unreasonable expectations created from fictionalized evidence collection and depicted investigative results in the hit TV show by the same name—I'm going to, respectfully, point out a few issues. I'm not a professional entertainment critic, but I've developed my own rating scale because I know the kind of scene that makes me want to throw a shoe.

Throughout *FBI Myths and Misconceptions: A Manual for Armchair Detectives,* in addition to breaking down clichés and reviewing FBI films and fiction, I'll be introducing you to a number of retired FBI agents I've interviewed, and sharing with you quotes and snippets from their episodes.

FBI PROFILERS HUNT SERIAL KILLERS

Serial Killers

FBI agents and FBI cases are often used as inspiration for writing fascinating thrillers and crime stories. However, if you were to place these fictional tales into distinct categories based on the more than two hundred violations of federal law under the Bureau's jurisdiction, a majority of the books, TV shows, and movies would fall under the category of "FBI profilers investigating serial killers."

Although serial murders are atypical of most murders and serial killers usually operate in a general geographic area, the proliferation of books and shows on the topic give the false impression that serial killers are roaming throughout the country one step ahead of the determined profilers hunting them. This is probably one of the most prevalent clichés about the FBI. I blame the public's fascination

11

with serial killers and FBI profilers on bestselling author Thomas Harris. *The Silence of the Lambs* is unquestionably one of the most popular thrillers about the FBI and serial killers. Jack Crawford, the FBI profiler character featured in Harris's novels was created after Harris attended classes at the FBI Academy taught by FBI agent John Douglas. Douglas was one of the pioneers of the Behavioral Science Unit (BSU), now known as the Behavioral Analysis Unit (BAU).

From the FBI Website

"Serial Murder"

Serial murder is a relatively rare event, estimated to comprise less than 1 percent of all murders committed in any given year. However, there is a macabre interest in the topic that far exceeds its scope and has generated countless articles, books, and movies. This public fascination began in the late 1880s, after a series of unsolved murders of sex workers occurred in the Whitechapel area of London committed by a still unknown individual who named himself "Jack the Ripper" and sent letters to the police claiming to be the killer.

(https://www.fbi.gov/stats-services/publications/serial-murder#one)

But *The Silence of the Lambs* is a blessing as well as a curse. Based on its success, serial killers plots are now a bona fide story genre. The CBS TV series *Criminal Minds* is also a testament to the genre's popularity. In addition to crime fiction and dramas, true crime books and movies have also capitalized on the popularity of serial killers, as have an abundant number of podcasts. These celebrity monsters are captivating a voracious audience and becoming almost an obsession for some true crime and horror fans. Several crime thriller authors have highly successful book series featuring FBI profilers as the central character.

Just the Facts

The FBI's involvement in serial killer cases has evolved under federal law. For example, the Bureau was authorized to investigate violent crimes against interstate travelers in 1994 and serial killings specifically in 1998. The FBI may investigate only when requested to do so by an appropriate law enforcement agency. Don't forget, serial killings are still local murders. Homicide detectives where the deaths occurred will remain actively involved in the investigation; the FBI works these cases with the cooperation and contributions of our local partners. The Bureau is also authorized to provide a variety of support services, from laboratory and behavioral analysis to crime statistics collection and the sharing of criminal identification information and history through our longstanding services and systems. However, as stated in the *Criminal Investigative Analysis: Practitioner Perspectives*, a four-part report written by J. Amber Scherer, MA, and John P. Jarvis, PhD, when they were assigned to FBI's Behavioral Research and Instruction Unit, the primary goal of criminal investigative analysis is to examine all of the behavioral information and provide advice to the requesting agency, rather than become involved in the actual investigative process. Obviously, the FBI's involvement in serial killer cases is complicated and multi-layered.

Consequently, serial killer novels and shows, no matter how well-written and entertaining, are inherently inaccurate. FBI profilers are not running down dark alleys or crawling around in dark basements hunting for serial killers. The primary goal of a profiler is to conduct behavioral analysis (also known as profiles) on unknown subjects, (known in FBI jargon as UNSUBS) in an attempt to discover additional information and clues to identify the person(s) responsible, assist in the resolution of hard-to-solve cases, and prevent future violence. The agents assigned to the BAU examine information submitted by one of the FBI field offices on behalf of or in coordination with a local law enforcement agency, and provide insight based on research and interviews regarding who might have committed the crime. Although they play an invaluable role in the investigative process, in most situations, FBI profilers are not actively involved in serial murder investigations. Dramatic scenes with profilers capturing a serial killer just before he murders his next victim are the Hollywood versions of how BAU profilers do their job.

I don't want to diminish the contributions of profilers in any way. The highly educated and trained FBI agents assigned as profilers to the BAU conduct important and comprehensive work, utilizing their education, training, and backgrounds in psychology and criminology. They review entire case files complete with investigative reports, crime scenes photos, and witness interviews, and they consult with investigators over the phone and occasionally in the field to provide a thorough assessment of the case. Before contacting a potential witness or source, agents may consult with a profiler to discuss the best way to approach the person and obtain their cooperation. Profilers may also suggest techniques that can encourage a suspect to provide a confession. Profilers are investigative tools for agents to use to solve cases. They may also interview victims and visit prisons to speak with serial killers responsible for similar crimes to gather criminal histories and analytics. The process of becoming an FBI profiler is highly competitive. Unlike in *The Silence of the Lambs*, rookies need not apply.

"Every one of the FBI's fifty-six field divisions has agents who we specifically train to be the liaison between the BAU and the local law enforcement agencies, and maybe even their own FBI office. They'll collect information and talk to the police officers involved in a case or their fellow agents, and they'll contact us and say, 'We think we have a good case for you,' and then that person will be brought on board, and we'll deal with the police officers or our own agents. And the case will work from there. So people like Ray Carr (agent profiler in the field) *were invaluable, certainly during my profiling career at the FBI. And they always knew how to put a case together and present just the facts we needed from them for us then to take it to the next level."*

—Retired agent and former BAU profiler Jim Fitzergerald in episode 003, "Forensic Linguistics and the Unabomber"

Agents in the field are often the first to learn about a difficult-to-solve case from a local law enforcement agency. They discuss the matter with the detective assigned to determine if it would be helpful to have the BAU review the file.

"When there's an unsolved homicide, an unsolved rape, an unsolved tampering with products, then threat assessments, kidnappings, expertise for search warrants, interview strategies—all these different things—are things that are worked out of the National Center for Analysis of Violent Crime down at Quantico. They

send agents from the field down there and train them. I had the opportunity not just to do a two-week stint down at Quantico, but I also went back for a four-week stint, and I went down for several other stints. Thirty days, at that time, working in the unit to hone my skills, allowing me to better serve the state and local police departments within the Philadelphia area. So, as they would bring cases to us, I would review them, get them ready, and then, in conjunction with Quantico, I would work those cases with the local police departments. The only cases brought to the unit are cases that the local and state agencies feel are unsolvable. So they're bringing it and asking for us to do an analysis, looking at the behavior that's occurred within the crime scene and the behavior exhibited by both the victim and the offender. So, although we can't give them a name, we can give them the type of person they should be looking for based on the interactions that occur within the crime scene. The opportunity and the chance is to make a difference; what everybody and all your listeners see on TV, what they watch, we get to live firsthand. It's like having a ticket to the greatest show on earth."

—Retired Agent Ray Carr episode 002, "Carl Gugasian, Tracking FBI's Most Prolific Bank Robber"

At any given time, there are fifteen to twenty full-time special agent profilers assigned to the BAU, working on developing criminal profiles for UNSUBS guilty of a variety of macabre violations. I worked as a special agent for twenty-six years, and I know of only two

FBI agents assigned cases involving serial killers. They worked in the field, not at Quantico. Currently, there are approximately 13,500 FBI agents, and I can assure you that 99 percent of them are not hunting serial killers—terrorists perhaps, but not serial killers.

————

However, there are agents who have had the opportunity to speak with some of the most infamous serial killers.

In episode 132, "Jeffrey Dahmer, Interrogating Serial Killers," retired agent Dan Craft talked about interviewing serial killer Jeffrey Dahmer four times and explained why he doesn't watch serial killer movies:

Jerri Williams (JW): When you watch TV or a movie or read a book about a serial killer, you see it has become its own genre. I look at serial killer crime fiction as similar to fantasy. There's so much about it that is over the top. Usually investigators find out about a serial killer after the fact after they've been caught. They're not chasing them down the street as they rack up one serial killing after another.

Dan Craft (DC): Sometimes, they do get them as suspects and the case agents are chasing them. It's not always after the fact. Sometimes, you can put a couple cases together, and when you can put the victim with the suspect all of a sudden it starts coming together and you try to catch them before they kill another one.

JW: I was talking primarily about when the investigator, the agent, is in harm's way. The serial killer is now after them, and as they're investigating, they're trying to evade and not be harmed by the serial killer. That usually doesn't happen.

DC: Yeah. Well, I don't watch that stuff on television. I lived it. I don't want to watch it. I don't read any of that. For one thing, it's not always accurate, but it is entertaining for some people. But I don't watch that and I don't read about it. I don't want to. I lived it. It's not exactly like it is on television. These victims are real. The worse part of this job is that we see the victims. It can be difficult.

FBI Film and Fiction Review

The Silence of the Lambs

The central characters in the bestselling author Thomas Harris's book *The Silence of the Lambs* and the 1991 Academy Award-winning movie (It won Best Picture, Director, Actor, Actress, and Adapted Screenplay) by the same name are FBI trainee Clarice Starling, her mentor FBI profiler Jack Crawford, and Dr. Hannibal Lecter, a former psychiatrist locked up in a high-security prison for the criminally insane. In the film, the roles are played by Jodie Foster, Scott Glenn, and Anthony Hopkins. *The Silence of the Lambs* is unquestionably one of the most popular novels and movies featuring the FBI and serial killers, a classic of the genre that illustrated the public's interest in being entertained by sadistic tales of serial murderers and the brave people who hunt them down.

Clarice Starling is summoned from her new agent training for a special assignment. Crawford asks her to interview Hannibal Lecter, not revealing that his true goal is to gain insight from Lecter regarding the identity of a serial killer known as "Buffalo Bill," who has kidnapped and murdered six women. The bizarre and troubling relationship that develops between Starling and Lecter is the primary focus of the story, along with Starling's allegiance to the FBI and Crawford, and the search for Buffalo Bill.

Thomas Harris's work developed into a highly successful franchise. *The Silence of the Lambs* is book two of the four-book Hannibal Lecter series. The other books in the series are *Red Dragon*, *Hannibal*, and *Hannibal Rising*. Each was adapted and made into a movie by the same name, in addition to a movie named *Manhunter* (which is the first film adaptation of the *Red Dragon* novel) and a TV series named *Hannibal*.

I remember watching this movie and being scared to death. I probably viewed most of the scary scenes with my hand partially covering my eyes and having to peek through my fingers. With all of its reality flaws, *The Silence of the Lambs* is the best book and movie of the genre.

My rating for *The Silence of the Lambs*: I kept my shoes on my feet, but during the movie, I loosened the laces just in case.

Mindhunter

The Netflix series *Mindhunter* (2017-) is a fictionalized version of the true crime book *Mindhunter: Inside the FBI's Elite Serial Crime Unit* by retired agent John Douglas and co-author Mark Olshaker. The main character in the TV show, FBI special agent and hostage negotiator Holden Ford, was inspired by the work and life of John Douglas. The show takes place in the 1970s, and Agent Ford believes he could enhance his negotiation skills if he could delve into the mind-set of the hostage takers, as well as applying this new-found knowledge to unsolved serial murder cases. The show's tag-line is, "How do we get ahead of crazy if we don't know how crazy thinks?"

Holden, along with his partner, FBI agent Bill Tench, and psychologist Wendy Carr, develop a program designed to allow investigators to anticipate the behaviors of unidentified serial killers by studying the actions of known violent criminals and the psychology of murder. Holden and Tench travel to facilities around the United States to interview incarcerated serial murderers about their crimes and motivations. In the TV show, the conversations the agents have with the serial killers were based on the recorded dialogue from FBI taped interviews with real-life murderers Edmund Kemper III, Montie Rissell, and Richard Speck. The TV series' storylines focus on the emotional effects their work has on Holden's and Tench's personal lives, as well as on their relationships with their FBI bosses. Agent Holden is played by actor Jonathan Groff, Holt McCallany plays Agent Tench, and Anna Torv stars as the consulting psychologist Wendy Carr.

A *New York Post* article dated October 21, 2017, references John Douglas's reaction, after he consulted on the Netflix miniseries: "'They're going by the book and I am very pleased. Watching the series is like reliving my life all over again.'"

Have you watched *Mindhunter* yet? In my opinion, it is one of the best TV crime dramas ever made about the FBI. I loved the fully developed characters and the fresh way the FBI agents interacted with loved ones and the violent deviant murderers they visited in prison.

My rating for *Mindhunter*: No footwear was removed during my viewing of this series, and all laces stayed tightly bound.

Criminal Minds

As of this writing, the popular TV series *Criminal Minds* (2005-2019) is in its fifteenth and final season. Here's a description of the show from the CBS website: "*Criminal Minds* revolves around an elite team of FBI profilers who analyze the country's most twisted criminal minds, anticipating their next moves before they strike again."

For the most part, each episode features a new predator, an UNSUB responsible for the latest heinous crime—who the team of profilers must identify, locate, and apprehend. With support from analysts assigned to the Behavioral Analysis Unit (BAU), the team, often risking their own lives, track leads that will help them solve the case.

I've never watched an entire episode of *Criminal Minds*. I'm not really into a weekly dose of serial killers and deviant sociopaths. No judgment, but it's just not the type of show I watch for entertainment. However, lots of viewers disagree with me. As I mentioned before, the series ran for fifteen seasons. So what do I know?

My rating for *Criminal Minds*: Has anyone seen my shoe?

THE FBI DOESN'T PLAY WELL WITH OTHERS

Law Enforcement Partners

How many movies have you seen where a local detective or sheriff is working on a case and the FBI shows up, is rude and condescending, and tries to take over the investigation? I'm sure you've watched that scene with a dour-faced and overbearing white male in a suit, in movies and cop shows like *Die Hard* and *Law & Order*. That is the worst. The storyline has been used for so long that it's self-perpetuating. Based on books and films, some police officers expect the FBI to come in and act this way. In real life, FBI agents meeting local law enforcement for the first time must deal with those stereotypes and the resulting resentment and suspicion before they can deal with the crime they're there to investigate. In those instances, agents must first break down resistance before they can do their jobs.

The Bureau doesn't "take over" cases from local agencies. The FBI has no hierarchical authority over local and state agencies. State and local law enforcement agencies are not subordinate to the FBI. If a crime occurs and the FBI shares jurisdiction with another agency or the FBI's assistance is requested, the FBI will work closely with local and state police in an informal partnership or, for certain cases, a task force is formed combining federal, state, and local resources and manpower to solve a crime or prevent one. In some situations, a Memorandum of Understanding (MOU) is drafted and signed by agency heads to establish responsibilities, financial obligations, and procedures.

"This (doesn't play well with others) stereotype is one that infects our relationships. When I first came into the FBI in the mid-80s, when I was working in New York City, this is something I battled from old seasoned detectives. I think that was a vestige of maybe the old days. But certainly, it's not the case anymore. I think writers use it as a weak way to bring conflict into their stories. Every story needs conflict, and this is a very weak cliché that some writers still rely on to bring in that conflict. But some of my best partners that I worked with in my whole career were detectives, and I maintain those friendships. When I was with the dive team, on at least two occasions I can tell you that the FBI dive team went into a high profile case made the recovery of the victim and never

told anybody we were there. We did the recovery and gave the credit to the local dive teams because it was their jurisdiction. We left town without ever taking credit, without ever letting the media and the public know we were there."

**—Retired agent Bobby Chacon, episode 008,
"Jamaican Gangs and FBI Dive Teams"**

Why do some writers tend to rely on this inaccurate portrayal? I understand it's used in an attempt to add conflict to a story. I'm aware that the number one rule of fiction is that it's not a story until something goes wrong. Yes, every story needs conflict, but writers should innovate the old cliché and create new and unique ideas to bring tension to their police procedurals and thrillers, instead of relying on this stale and false scenario. During my career, I worked primarily economic crime cases, and my subjects were frequently charged with wire and mail fraud. That meant that I often worked with United States postal inspectors; some of my best investigative partners were postal inspectors. I maintain those friendships to this day.

That's not to say that there are never any turf wars where federal agencies fight to maintain lead jurisdiction over certain investigations. The FBI is the United States' primary law enforcement agency, with enforcement of more than two hundred categories of federal laws. Other federal agencies, such as the Internal Revenue Service (IRS), the Drug Enforcement Agency (DEA), the Postal Inspection Service (USPIS), and the Bureau of Alcohol, Tobacco, Firearms and Explosives (ATF), are single-mission agencies charged with enforcing specific violations and laws. Where concurrent jurisdiction may exist, the FBI works closely with these other agencies to ensure there is no duplication of effort or complications due to miscommunication.

Although most jurisdictional issues can be reasonably resolved with agency heads sitting around a conference room table, that does not mean past disagreements have not resulted in dire consequences for the United States. The FBI and the Central Intelligence Agency (CIA) failing to share vital intelligence, and it having an impact on our national security, has been documented in numerous books and films as a leading factor in the tragic events that unfolded on 9/11. Those lessons, hopefully, have been learned and resolved.

The FBI has embraced the task force concept since the early 1980s, collaborating with other federal, state, and local law enforcement agencies for combating violent crime and drug activity, as well as terrorism threats. Task forces have proven to be an efficient method for agencies to tackle specific crime and national security concerns together. Violent Gang Safe Streets Task Forces and Joint Terrorism

Task Forces (JTTF) throughout the country bring together the resources and manpower of all the agencies combined. FBI agents respect and value the contributions other agencies bring to the table and strive to maintain collaborative relationships with all law enforcement partners. The FBI's relationship with its law enforcement counterparts has been built on years of mutual respect and collaboration.

In episode 007, "Tracking Top Ten Fugitives" retired agent Jeff Covington spoke about working in the early to mid-1990s on the Philadelphia Division Fugitive Task Force with local and state law enforcement partners:

Jeff Covington: There was a need for the FBI to team up with some of our local partners to try to put a dent in the exploding amount of violent crime. Philadelphia SAC (Special Agent in Charge) Bob Reutter brought the program to the Philadelphia FBI Office. We partnered up with the Major Crimes Unit of the Philadelphia Police Department, with the Court Warrant Unit from the Philadelphia Court of Common Pleas, and the Pennsylvania State Police. We all sign memorandums of understanding, and each one of those guys was sworn in as a Special United States Marshal, so they could have all the powers of the FBI. Partners were made up of an FBI agent and a law enforcement member in about eight teams, and they could go anywhere. If we went over to New

Jersey, they could go. If we went down to Delaware or Baltimore, they could go. That designation of *Special United States Marshal* allowed them to carry their guns and have the same powers that their FBI partners had.

It was good in a lot of ways, debunking that myth that the FBI can't work with other people. Also, they had resources. They had warrants they supplied us with, they had sources, and they had the local influence we needed. Even though the FBI is big and powerful, we can't do everything.

Ninety percent of our warrants came from those units, the State Police, the Court Warrant Unit, and Major Crimes. Also, these guys knew the turf, and that was probably one of the biggest things. They knew their way around the city. If we had a problem, they could get (patrol) cars out to us. And it also fostered a good sense, not only with us but with the public, that law enforcement can work together. At one point, there were fifty-thousand unserved violent crime warrants on the books, and nobody was looking for those guys. Local and state law enforcement didn't have the manpower to do it. The task force was designed to put a dent in those things. And believe me, we did.

We went to firearms training together. Each of us went to a Safe Streets school-teaching situation, so we could build up the professionalism of the task force and make it into a unit that was actually quite formidable. One guy turned himself in when he heard that the task force was looking for him. We developed a good reputation: You don't mess with the Philadelphia Fugitive Task Force. You're better off turning yourself in."

———

The task force concept is a win-win for all participating agencies.

In episode 069, "Triple Murder, Safe Streets Task Force," retired agent Gina Davis talked about supervising a Safe Streets Task Force and the advantages working as a team with multiple agencies provides to law enforcement:

Gina Davis: This is the beauty of the Safe Streets Task Force and any kind of FBI sponsored task force: we have the ability to use not only the federal legal system, but we also have the ability to use the state and the local jurisdictions as well to get process on our criminals.

The FBI uses the Safe Streets Task Force program as a way to assist local jurisdictions with specific crime problems that sometimes need the abilities and the resources of the FBI and other law enforcement agencies to address. So, back in 1992, we started our first Safe Streets Task Forces and currently the FBI probably has more than 150 of them across the country. What the Safe Streets Task Forces do is go to their local police departments, identifying agencies and personnel that would fit well together to address a specific violent crime problems. It could be fugitives, gang violence, or drug trafficking. The task force that we started in the Baltimore Division was a Safe Streets Task Force addressing violent crime and cold case homicides. We had a mixture of local police officers from the county, we also had a couple of auxiliary members from other jurisdictions, and we had some folks from the state police in Maryland. The FBI pays the overtime associated with the police officers who work on the task force. We worked as a team. And basically it's a way to augment the resources of both departments.

They are deputized. They go through the same background investigation that special agents go through. They receive a top secret security clearance and they have access to FBI records and report systems. They also have access to FBI vehicles and FBI equipment to work the joint investigations. The other important fact about the task force officers is that they really are under the supervision of the FBI. On some occasions, we will deputize supervisors from the other departments to work on the team. Depending upon the size of the task force, you might have an FBI supervisor and a local supervisor working with the task force. However, the majority of the time, everyone is under the FBI's supervision.

FBI Film and Fiction Review

The Looming Tower

Written by Lawrence Wright, this Pulitzer Prize-winning nonfiction book about the rise of al-Qaeda details the intelligence failures that culminated in the attacks on the World Trade Center. It was re-created in 2018 as a ten-episode TV drama. The series traces the rivalry between the FBI and CIA in the late 1990s, in the midst of the growing threat of terrorist activity from al-Qaeda at the direction of Osama Bin Laden. The inter-agency conflict depicted in *The Looming Tower* is alleged to have been responsible for both agencies missing the many clues that indicated the tragedy of 9/11 was imminent. The series portrays real-life FBI agent John O'Neill, who was in charge of the FBI's counter-terrorism unit in New York and Muslim American agent Ali Soufan. Both agents are featured by name in the series and are played by Jeff Daniels and French actor Tahar Rahim.

No footwear was removed while watching *The Looming Tower*. All laces stayed tightly tied.

Retired agent Ali Soufan in episode 154, "USS Cole Bombing, The Black Banners," shared his thoughts about having an actor portray him on the Hulu TV series The Looming Towers:

Jerri Williams (JW): I have to ask you: What did you think about the series, and what was it like to have someone play you? The actor who played you was so good. I kind of had a little crush on him. He was so vulnerable.

Ali Soufan (AS): I will let him know that.

JW: Yes, please do. (laughs)

AS: Yeah, I think Tahar (Rahim) did a phenomenal job, and I think overall the Hulu series kept true to the spirit of the story. Definitely they put some drama here and there.

JW: The firefight in the street and through the apartment complex I thought was a little over the top.

AS: Yeah, I mean they put in some drama. But that's normal with Hollywood. But when it comes to the spirit of the story, I think they kept true to their word that they wanted to stay factual. I think it's always weird for me to watch it because, as a person who lived through a lot of these kind of things and knows many of these characters, I would like to… You know, in our minds especially as FBI agents, we like to have only the facts, right? So we don't have a place for the drama. We don't have a place for exaggerations. We don't have a place for any of these kind of things. So every time I see it, the needle is going crazy up and down, up and down. "No, no that's not exactly what happened." I am the worst person to watch the series with. But overall, I think I agree with you. They did a good job.

MOST FBI AGENTS ARE WHITE MALES, & FEMALE AGENTS ARE SINGLE

Special Agent Statistics

Although recent books, TV shows, and movies portray the FBI as a highly diverse organization, the old image of white men in dark suits is still somewhat accurate. Approximately 70 percent of special agents are white males, so this cliché of only white male agents is not too off the mark. However, I included this statement as a cliché because the demographics are changing. Slowly. FBI agents are not confined to the cookie cutter models from central casting portrayed in years past. Currently, out of approximately 13,500 total special agents, the workforce also includes 19 percent women, 17 percent minorities, as well as individuals of different religions and sexual orientations.

During my time in the Bureau, when I told people what I did for a living, my announcement was usually met with raised eyebrows and a confused stare because, as an African American woman, I didn't look like an FBI agent. It didn't help that I also joined when minorities made up 8.1 percent and women made up less than 5.8 percent of the special agent ranks. Currently, black women make up less than 1 percent. By the way, black women made up 0.3 percent when I received my appointment in 1982. I was one of twenty-three black women out of the 8,270 agents serving in the Bureau at the time.

All law enforcement agencies should reflect the population they serve and the FBI is actively recruiting more women and minorities. I'm always in recruitment mode. If you or someone you know meets the basic qualifications— a minimum of a bachelor's degree, between twenty-three and thirty-seven years of age, and a U.S. citizen— please consider applying for a special agent position.

Women and minority agents have been appointed to leadership roles in the FBI. At the time of the publication of *FBI Myths and Misconceptions: A Manual for Armchair Detectives*, an informal review of the fifty-six FBI field offices indicated that the assistant director in charge (ADIC) of the Washington Field Office was a woman, and eight of the other FBI field offices were also led by women. The number of minority special agents in charge (SACs) was also eight. Among them was one minority female SAC. This review did not include senior executive service (SES) positions at FBI Headquarters.

TV shows that are helping to change the stereotype are *Criminal Minds*, where the BAU unit chief is a woman, *FBI* on CBS, where the SAC character is a woman, and *Designated Survivor*, where the assistant director is an African American male and the lead case agent is an Asian American woman. These series help to promote the FBI to eligible men and women who may not have otherwise considered the FBI as a career choice. These TV shows introduce the FBI to more potential candidates than a college career day or job fair presentation. It's exciting to imagine viewers watching those characters and thinking to themselves, *Maybe I can do that too*.

However, I suspect that some women do not consider joining the FBI as a special agent because female FBI characters are often depicted as unattached and childless. The only thing she has in her life is her job. Applicants may wonder where a family would fit in. Seldom do you see female and male agent characters dropping their children off at daycare or preparing a healthy meal for their families. The typical female agent in movies and TV shows is portrayed as single in relationships and singular in focus. Married women candidates or those looking to one day have a life that includes a spouse and kids may not believe the position will work with the demands of raising a family.

On the contrary, most veteran female agents, like their male counterparts, are married and have children. It can be done. But like any other high-pressure position, it requires support to navigate the long days with unpredictable hours and out-of-town travel. Granted, it is easier for writers not to have to address life outside of the FBI office if they make agents single and childless.

In writing my crime fiction series featuring FBI agent Kari Wheeler, I made sure to enhance and, yes, complicate the development of her character arc by giving her a not-thrilled-about-her-job husband and three active kids at home. During my FBI career, I raised three kids while on the job. Admittedly, this was possible because my husband, a high school history teacher, took up the slack when I needed to get into work early, stay late or travel on assignment. He was also home with the kids every summer. Being an FBI agent with a family can work. Understanding and supportive spouses, as well as a community in the form of relatives, friends, and neighbors, are the keys to success.

I also worked on a squad where I managed my own cases. That meant, for the most part, that I decided when I needed to interview a witness, execute a search, or make an arrest (never on parent-teacher conference days or sports event nights). Things get complicated when you are assigned to a squad or task force where decisions are made for the team. The FBI has excellent benefits for their employees including vacation time and paid holidays. No matter where you are assigned around the country, you'll be able to take off time to visit your family and friends.

Another inaccurate portrayal of agents who are women involves the overemphasis of the physical attributes of the actresses portraying them. On the ABC series *Quantico*, the lead character, Special Agent Alex Parrish, seemed always to be wearing low-cut and tight-fitting clothes. In the real world, all agents wear attire appropriate for the specific work environment. Women do not have to look or act like the guys, but if there's an arrest or a search, they'll be sporting the blue nylon raid jacket with the gold FBI letters, khakis pants, sneakers, and the baseball cap too. And when it's time to go to the office or testify in court, the female agents will be wearing an appropriate business suit or dress topped with a jacket to conceal their guns. I can assure you that instructions on distracting bad guys with your cleavage are not covered in the training sessions taught at the Academy.

History of Diversity in the FBI

The following post, prepared for the FBI's 100th anniversary, appears on the FBI website:

From the FBI Website

"FBI 100: The Top Ten Myths in FBI History," Myth #5: There were no minority agents during the Hoover years.

The FBI was hardly way ahead of its time in providing equal career opportunities to all Americans, but it is not true that the FBI was unwilling to hire minorities during Hoover's tenure…or (as one variation of the myth goes) was reluctant to hire minority agents until ordered to do so by President Kennedy in the early 1960s. The fact is, many minority special agents worked in the FBI from the early 1920s forward. An African-American agent named James Amos, for example, investigated major cases in New York from 1921 to 1953, while the Striders—an African-American father/son agent team in Los Angeles—served with distinction from the 1940s through the early 1970s. Hispanic Agent Manuel Sorola served in a number of our western offices from the 1920s through the 1940s, and Filipino-born Agent Flaviano Guerrero served ably in the 1940s. All told, there were dozens of minority special agents on our rolls before Hoover died in 1972.

(https://archives.fbi.gov/archives/news/stories/2008/july/myths_072408)

It should be noted that most of the minority agents mentioned in the section above were hired during the period when agents were not required to have a college degree or attend FBI training academy which opened in the 1940s on Marine Corps Base Quantico, Virginia. Once the new formalized recruitment and training criteria were established, twenty years followed before minority agents were hired and welcomed at the academy. I respect the contributions of the brave men who had worked as special agents before these changes, but I'm not inclined to ignore the discriminatory practices and disparate treatment that existed during the early days of the Bureau. It is a fact that prior to 1962, the FBI hired no "fully qualified" African American special agents and Director Hoover was under pressure by Attorney General Robert F. Kennedy and the Department of Justice to diversify the professional federal law enforcement ranks of the FBI. Several African American support employees had been given the title of "Special Agent" even though they did not meet the college requirements, were not allowed to attend the FBI Academy, and were not allowed to perform many of the duties described in the special agent job description. The first two fully qualified and college-educated African American candidates to attend the FBI Academy, Aubrey Lewis and James Barrow, entered on duty together in the summer of 1962. A year later in the summer of 1963, Wayne Davis and another African American candidate, John Cary, attended the FBI Academy and joined the Bureau.

In episode 014, "Director Hoover and FBI Diversity," retired agent Wayne Davis spoke about being one of the first African American agents hired in the early 1960s, the history of diversity in the FBI, and its importance:

Wayne Davis: (Before I received my appointment to the FBI), Director Hoover was under a lot of pressure to diversify his special agent force. There were a lot of minorities in clerical or what we now call 'professional support positions.' But minorities in the agent workforce were severely lacking, and Mr. Hoover really wasn't making any efforts in that regard. Bobby Kennedy was the attorney general, and he made it very difficult for Hoover not to do what he wanted Hoover to do in the area of minority hiring. Bobby Kennedy was attempting to diversify the ranks of the Department of Justice in general, and the FBI in particular.

At the time, there were no fully qualified, school trained, minority special agents. There were about five or six or seven individuals who, through their length of service, carried special agent credentials. But they didn't really have the full qualifications that agents are required to have. They did not have the college education, nor did they attend the FBI

Academy. I can name them. Jimmy Young worked 42-classifications, the (military) deserter cases. When Director Hoover came to New York, Jimmy was his chauffeur. When the pressure and the heat was on the director, he named Jimmy Young as a special agent. But the work that Jimmy did was very limited. There was another fellow in New York, Harold Carr, who got special agent credentials, again because of long and loyal service and so Director Hoover could check that box. Harold Carr stayed down in the basement of the building and kept the director's limousine polished. In Chicago, there was Karl Mason. It was the same story; Karl Mason did limited investigative work, had no college education, and drove the director should he have to go to Chicago. Miami, the same story—Leo McClaren did the same job. In Los Angeles, it was the Striders, Jesse Strider and his son, Bob. They did investigative work, but they also drove the director when he came out, maybe to go to the track at San Diego. But that was the extent pretty much of black special agents. They carried credentials, didn't have the full qualifications, but did what they had to do.

Those who were in the field offices did do some limited investigative work. I spoke with Jimmy Young on several occasions because I had to go to New York to work on a special assignment. We got a chance to talk with Jimmy then. Jimmy felt good. He wore a suit and tie, and he did do the job. But it's interesting though. They sent me in (to New York) for the special, and I teamed up with another fellow who they sent in from Miami named James Barrow. They didn't send out Jimmy Young to do these things that they were asking Jim Barrow and me to do, because we had the qualifications, we could write the reports, and we could contact the informants and everything. I think the fellows who were not fully qualified but carried the special agent credentials felt good about seeing the new breed.

In 1962, the first two fully qualified African Americans were hired. One was Aubrey Lewis and also in his class was James Barrow. James "Jim" Barrow had been a clerical employee in the New York office who had the education and had worked for the three years required to pass the examinations. Aubrey Lewis, I believe, was teaching in Montclair, New Jersey, at the time. But Aubrey Lewis was an All-American athlete, graduate of Notre Dame University, and all-star football player and track star. So, he had that as part of his credentials, so to speak. When the FBI hired him, they sent him to training school. That was 1962 and *Ebony* magazine had an article on him. Poor Jim Barrow didn't even get his face in the picture. But Lewis was the star, the poster boy. He was a nice-looking fellow and the whole nine yards. So, those were the first two that went into class in the summer of 1962. Yours truly and another fellow named John Cary came through the following year. During that whole year (after hiring Lewis and Barrow) they weren't able to find anyone else, apparently, that Hoover liked to go through training school. So John Cary and Wayne Davis were the second (set) to go through the FBI Academy in Quantico, Virginia.

FBI agents are the people who are out there on the street, talking to people, developing sources of information, being that first line for people who probably have never met an FBI agent. With this country being as diverse as it is, my feeling is that's reason enough for the FBI special agent position to reflect the diversity in this country."

History of Women in the FBI

Most are under the impression that there were no female special agents before or during Hoover's tenure as the director of the FBI. However, that's not correct.

Only Female Agent Hired by Hoover Was Assigned to Philadelphia

Historical accounts refer to 1972 as the year of the "first female FBI agents." Although that term is technically correct, there were three female agents in the Bureau of Investigation in the 1920s. When J. Edgar Hoover took over the Bureau of Investigation in 1924 (later to be renamed the Federal Bureau of Investigation), there were two female special agents on duty. They resigned shortly after that, but another female agent, appointed in November 1924, served until 1928.

Lenore Houston applied for the position of special agent of the Bureau of Investigation in June of 1922. She received glowing recommendations and on January 14, 1924, Bureau Director William Burns appointed her a special employee. Her salary was to be $7 per day, plus $4 a day instead of subsistence when absent from her office of assignment in Philadelphia. She handled White Slave Law violations. At the time she entered on duty she was forty-five years old and single. She was a high school graduate, had three years of college, and had completed a business course.

Congressman William Graham wrote to Director Burns on several occasions to urge that Special Employee Houston be designated a special agent. On November 6, 1924, Hoover took his advice and notified the appointment clerk to make the change. During her time at the Philadelphia Office, Miss Houston received excellent performance ratings. She also earned many salary increases, and by April 1, 1927, her yearly income was $3,100.

On August 29, 1927, Miss Houston transferred to the Washington Field Office, where, allegedly, her work got steadily worse. On October 20, 1928, she was placed on leave without pay through November 7, at which time her resignation was effective. A report dated December 30, 1930, indicated that Miss Houston had been confined to a hospital suffering from hallucinations and threatened to shoot Hoover as soon as she was released.

It would be forty-six years later, and just days after Hoover's death, before women would be allowed to serve the FBI again as special agents.

In the FBI's early days, women served almost exclusively in traditional jobs as secretaries and file clerks. During wartime, women in the FBI, like everywhere else in America, began to train and work in positions previously dominated by men. By 1948, one-third of the FBI's employees were women, a fact that surprised those who thought of the FBI as strictly male. Women held technical and complex positions, and at times, they volunteered to help out male agents by posing as their dinner dates or by eavesdropping on conversations in ladies' rooms. In the 1950s, women began to show a real interest in becoming special agents, but the Bureau's policy prohibited their hiring, citing a need for a streamlined force, hazards on the job, and problems associated with transfers.

Change was slow in coming as illustrated in an excerpt from a 1971 Bureau policy statement:

"It is not the intent of the FBI to confine (the special agent position) to males without there being very good reasons to do so…lurking in the minds of those bent on defying the law must be the ever-present concern for the prowess and the ability of the FBI agent…the response by our agents must be quick and is frequently military in nature with one man, supported by others, making the initial move, such as bounding into a room…he must create the impression that he is intrepid, forceful, aggressive, dominant, and resolute, our work involves basically man against man and is a body contact profession."

After a lawsuit and a series of executive orders, and just nine days after Mr. Hoover's death, the policy also expired. (The above paragraphs are edited excerpts from a narrative on the history of the Philadelphia Division compiled by a former Philadelphia Chief of Clerks)

That must have been a relief for the many women who had received the following letter forwarded to them from FBI Headquarters less than a year before:

Dear Miss _____,

I am glad to learn from your letter received on (date) that you are interested in a career in the FBI and enclosed are publications regarding the opportunities available and the requirements for employment with us.

Because of the nature of the duties, our Special Agents are called upon to perform, we do not employ women in this position. We must have Agents who are qualified to cope with any situation they may face. As you will see, however, women do hold many important positions in this Bureau.

Sincerely yours,
John Edgar Hoover
Director

Among the FBI's first female agents in modern times were a former nun, Joanne Pierce, and a marine, Sue Roley. With their unique backgrounds, it appeared that the only thing they had in common was that they were at least five feet seven inches tall, a height requirement which was not lifted for male and female agents until three years later. During my Bureau career, I was often the first female FBI agent most people had ever met. It is perplexing to me that law enforcement is still considered a non-traditional career for a woman.

Being the "first" women agents must have been challenging for Pierce and Roley. If I'm honest, I must admit that my early days in the Bureau weren't always easy. I joined the FBI at a time when everyone was still getting used to female agents. I could share some eyebrow-raising war stories. Fortunately, in spite of my shaky beginnings, it had no effect on what I was able to accomplish during my career. When you're trying to make a name for yourself and create a positive reputation in a job where there are very few women, you are aware that you have the responsibility of saying and doing things that will, hopefully, help the women coming up behind you.

A female agent will no longer be considered a novelty when women are fully integrated into the law enforcement workforce. Currently, women hold only 12–15 percent of policing positions, even though more than half of medical school and law school students are women, two equally demanding professions once considered off-limits to women. But law enforcement is still not a widely preferred career choice for women. Being a successful woman in the FBI and other local, state, and federal agencies, surrounded by men, requires the usual police skills, and fitness, but above all else, it takes determination and confidence in one's abilities.

But success in law enforcement for a woman is not being one of the boys. It's being one of the team. It is not important that you get invited to go out to a club or play a pickup game of basketball after work. What's important is that you get invited along on interviews and arrests. Of course, if you're the case agent, you get to do the inviting.

FBI Film and Fiction Review

Wind River

This 2017 feature film is a crime thriller about a female FBI agent who teams up with a veteran tracker with the Fish and Wildlife Service. Together, they, with the assistance of the local tribal police department work to investigate the rape and murder of a young Native American woman on a Wyoming reservation. The movie follows FBI agent Jane Banner, apparently single and childless, who is assigned solo to solve this crime, as a highly competent investigator who knows how to handle herself. The movie stars Elizabeth Olsen and Jeremy Renner.

Although there are a few things the movie gets wrong, the fact that Agent Banner was sent out alone is not one of them. There are FBI agents throughout the country who are assigned to represent the FBI's interest in remote areas. Those agents rely on their relationships with local law enforcement for backup and assistance. In *Wind River*, it is explained that Agent Banner arrived from Las Vegas to investigate the young woman's murder. In real life, an agent would not have been dispatched from the Las Vegas Division, but instead from one of the four satellite offices or resident agencies; Cheyenne, Casper, Lander, and Jackson Hole, within the Denver Division's Wyoming territory.

Another misconception the movie makes involves the numerous gun battles Agent Banner encounters. In an actual situation where a Bureau weapon is discharged, the FBI would have immediately deployed a shooting review team to investigate, especially when there are fatalities and an agent is shot. I explain more about shooting incidents in the Chapter #14, where I discuss agents being involved in gun battles. In spite of these inaccuracies, I found *Wind River* to be entertaining and recommend you watch the movie if you haven't yet seen it.

My rating for *Wind River*: I kept my shoes on my feet, but during the show, I loosened the laces just in case.

Miss Congeniality 1 & 2

This comedy, released in 2000, features Sandra Bullock in the title role of Gracie Hart, a female FBI agent who goes undercover as a contestant in the Miss United States beauty pageant in order to bring down a terrorist threatening to bomb the pageant. Single and childless, Gracie is as far from being a beauty queen as one can get. Her basic beauty routine is washing her face and maybe brushing her hair. She is not the type to be concerned about putting on make-up or wearing pretty dresses. However, when the investigation requires an agent to join the competition as a participant, Agent Hart gets a make-over, becomes a contestant, and eventually solves the case.

In *Miss Congeniality 2* (2005), Gracie Hart (Sandra Bullock once more) is asked to be the FBI spokesperson for yet another case centered around the Miss United States beauty pageant. This time Miss United States and the pageant's host are kidnapped. Agent Hart is reluctantly teamed up with Agent Sam Fuller (played by Regina King), a female FBI agent who has anger management issues, and they fly out to Las Vegas to rescue the kidnappers' victims.

These two films are not the only comedies where Sandra Bullock played a "I'm just one of the boys" female FBI agent. She played a similar role in *Heat* costarring Melissa McCarthy who also portrayed a unkempt, disgruntled female cop, but with a much better love life.

Yes, these films are comedies and actually pretty funny. However, the female law enforcement stereotypes were on overload in these three movies. Single? Check. Acts like one of the guys? Check. Childless? Check. Most agents, whether male or female, are employed in a managerial level position before joining the FBI and know how to carry themselves in a professional manner. No wonder women are hesitant to consider law enforcement as a career if these are the images presented to them. Not very attractive (pun intended) role models.

My rating for *Miss Congeniality*: Has anyone seen my shoe?

#4 THE FBI ONLY HIRES ACCOUNTANTS, ATTORNEYS, POLICE, & MILITARY OFFICERS

Unexpected Agent

Early in the FBI's history when agents investigated mostly white-collar and civil rights cases, agents with legal and accounting backgrounds were preferred. Much later, as the Bureau acquired additional violations under its jurisdiction—such as bank robbery, organized crime, and illegal drugs—candidates with experience and degrees in criminal justice were also sought. Currently, the FBI's recruitment efforts for special agent positions target candidates from a wide variety of backgrounds. People working everyday jobs, such as teachers, nurses, sales managers, linguists, cyber/computer specialists, pilots, and engineers are encouraged to apply to the FBI. I was a juvenile probation officer with a bachelor's in psychology before I was hired. The Bureau is in particular need of candidates working in STEM (science, technology, engineering, and mathematics) fields. These individuals are ideal for FBI positions involving forensic science, computer technology, cybersecurity, electronic surveillance, biometrics, and encryption. You might be surprised to learn that there are agents in the FBI who were employed as dentists, medical doctors, and scientists before joining. There are even a few former professional athletes.

The FBI is looking for hardworking and self-motivated individuals. If there were times in your life when you had to overcome obstacles and successfully persevered, these are things to note during your panel interview, as well as your current accomplishments. Candidates should be prepared to review the FBI Core Competencies[*] and evaluate their life experiences with regard to what the Bureau expects from employees. Investigators will conduct a background investigation for applicants being considered for the special agent position, the best predictor of future behavior is past behavior. Depending on how long you've been out of college, former professors will be interviewed, in addition to recommendations from current and previous employers, associates, and neighbors.

---

[*]   https://www.fbijobs.gov/sites/default/files/FBI_Core_Competencies_Definitions.pdf

If you are looking into the FBI before obtaining the required four-year bachelor's degree, I encourage you to major in a degree program that is of most interest to you. If that's criminal justice, then by all means major in criminal justice. If you think you might like accounting, then please go for a degree in accounting. But none of us know what the future may hold. You don't want to end up in an industry that you only entered because you are trying to become an agent with the FBI. There are many individuals in law enforcement who see the FBI as the next step, the next level. Therefore, obtaining a minor or gaining expertise in an area that you truly enjoy could make you more competitive, such as fluent language skills, intelligence gathering, or experience in forensics. But certainly consider majoring in any of the degree programs offered at accredited universities. The FBI is looking for candidates from all disciplines.

Competitive candidates for the special agent position, are working in positions with managerial responsibilities and perhaps a few direct reports. It's not your job title that matters. Make sure you're the best at what you do. Make sure you shine and stand out among your peers and coworkers.

Age and Other Basic Requirements

Some TV shows and films cast actors who appear to be too young or too old for the role of an FBI agent.

Although the qualifying age to join the FBI is twenty-three, the average new agent is thirty years old and has worked a managerial-level position for several years before receiving an appointment to the FBI Academy. FBI characters in film and fiction would be portrayed more accurately as more seasoned and experienced but not too old. The mandatory retirement age for federal law enforcement officers is fifty-seven, though an agent can receive a limited extension up to the age of sixty if his or her continued service is in the public's interest. Most agents, however, retire from the FBI in their early fifties to start post-FBI positions while they're still marketable (ageism exists, even for FBI agents). I retired when I was fifty-one.

I enjoyed watching a TV show on TNT network called *Good Behavior*, starring Michelle Dockery and Juan Diego Botto. A recurring character, FBI Agent Rhonda Lashever, was portrayed as cynical, sarcastic, and just plain rude. Ann Dowd, the actress who played her, although perfect for the refreshingly unique part in every other way, seemed too old for the role. During one of the episodes, when the character remarked that she was sixty-two years old, my assessment was validated. Sixty-two? She should have retired five years earlier. This bitter and disgruntled FBI character was hanging onto her job by a thin thread. No one would have granted her an extension.

Why does it matter? Because hundreds of thousands of people who watched *Good Behavior* now have inaccurate info about the retirement age for FBI agents. If you are writing a book or you're producing a movie about an FBI agent, the characters shouldn't be too young or too old. For anyone who knows the real age requirements, it's going to take their focus away from the screen or off the page.

In addition to the age and educational requirements, candidates must be a U.S. citizen, be able to obtain a top secret SCI (sensitive compartmented information) clearance, and comply with the FBI drug policy. To learn more about the qualifications and employment requirements to apply for the special agent position, visit FBIJobs.gov.

FBI Film and Fiction Review

Quantico

The TV series *Quantico* ran for three strangely unconnected seasons (2015-2018). The show followed Alex Parrish (played by Priyanka Chopra), during the first few years of her mercurial time as a special agent, starting with her time at the FBI Academy in Quantico. Upon, graduating with a bright and productive career ahead of her, she instead becomes the prime suspect in a deadly terrorist attack that takes place at Grand Central Station in New York City. The second half of the first season has Alex trying to prove that she is innocent with help from her new agent classmates.

I joke that whenever I attempted to watch Quantico, I kept getting distracted by Alex's beautiful thick, wavy hair or by the nagging questions I had regarding why her uniform tops were tighter and cut lower than any of the other female trainees in her class. But regardless of those diversions, for the most part, in season one I found that the agent interactions and the FBI Academy were portrayed as bright, shiny, exaggerated versions of the real thing, with the following corrections:

- FBI new agent trainees are not called NATS (pronounced *gnats*).

- New agent trainees are not all young and good-looking. The FBI prefers to hire individuals with several years of work experience, which means a new agent training class might have several older people—up to thirty-seven years of age. Also, the FBI has no policy against hiring unattractive people.

- Having sex with classmates either on or off campus is prohibited.

- New agents are expected to respect the personal property of classmates. Sneaking into classmates' rooms to gather intelligence about their past indiscretions by removing files and downloading data from laptops is neither condoned or necessary. After the thorough backgrounds conducted on each trainee, no secrets are left to be revealed.

Season one introduced the FBI to a new and diverse generation of boys and girls who now dream of becoming FBI agents when they grow up. But season two's CIA infiltration and season three's black ops plots crossed into the land of make-believe and didn't bother to portray anything close to how the real FBI works.

My rating for *Quantico*: Has anyone seen my shoe?

#5 ONE AGENT CAN WORK A MAJOR INVESTIGATION ALONE

A Career Like No Other

Often, due to time constraints, writers don't have the luxury of developing multiple characters. Instead, they create one composite character to represent a few different players. It would be impossible to recognize all of the individuals involved in a real life major investigation; creating an accurate portrayal of each participant is an unachievable task if the case must be solved within an hour to two hours. So even though it takes a team to work a major investigation, books, TV shows, and movies are written to allow the main character to portray the roles of several agents, giving the impression that one agent can conduct an entire investigation by herself. However, during a major investigation in the field, assistance with surveillances, searches, arrests, monitoring wiretaps, transcribing tapes, and more is always needed. An entire squad or office gets involved and plays a part in the success of the operation. As the saying goes, it takes a village.

Composite characters are a major complaint of FBI agents watching and reading these crime stories that dramatize a true FBI event. Time constraints dictate that one actor portray one agent on the case but is shown conducting parts of the investigation that were conducted by others in real life. I can imagine that is hurtful and frustrating to see the contributions of co-workers (or yourself) ignored, but that's the entertainment business. It may be surprising to learn that when agents sell the rights to their life stories, they often lose the ability to object to creative changes made. A case where nary a gun shot was fired in real life, might have the agent involved in several firefights during the fictionalized version.

When real cops watch cop shows, it can also be annoying for them to see agents and police officers acting like Rambo, battling teams of bad guys. Confronting multiple armed suspects alone goes against all logical law enforcement tactics and arrest procedures. (That's not to say that there aren't any hot shot agents in the FBI who believe they are saviors of the universe; in the FBI, we call them "blue flamers," usually young agents so eager and energetic that, similar to rocket at launch, they have fire shooting from their backsides.) However implausible, if writers believe it's what their audience wants, then those scenes will always be included in the script.

Case Agents, File Reviews, and Sources

Another irritation is when an agent on TV appears to be assigned to work every violation under the Bureau's jurisdiction with no distinction regarding what squad they're on. FBI agents are assigned to squads based on related federal violations. I admit to a small infraction of this issue. In my FBI Philadelphia corruption squad series featuring Special Agent Kari Wheeler, she's assigned both economic crime and public corruption cases, even though in the real Philadelphia Division these would be violations worked on two different squads. I wrote the novels this way because I want Kari, my main character, to be able to work a variety of fraud and corruption cases, regardless if the crimes were committed by individuals, corporations, or public servants and officials. So I guess am guilty of squad blending too.

Most squads have ten to thirty agents working under one supervisory special agent (SSA). Although agents will need some support to work their investigations, every case has a case agent who is primarily responsible for the administration of the entire investigation. On non-task force squads, agents work alone. They'll team up with a squad mate for corroboration and safety concerns. However, the FBI requires agents to assume an almost entrepreneurial ownership of their cases. Each assignment is like running a business. FBI agents must figure out the manpower and resources needed, and there's no one standing over them checking on their daily progress and making sure they are doing their jobs. Every day, they get to decide what they're going to do. It's a remarkable freedom that requires tremendous self-discipline and motivation. Every ninety days, the squad supervisor reviews the agents' case files, looking for documentation that they are pulling their weight. This is one of the primary reasons the average age of new agents trainees is thirty years old—the bureau is looking for people who can hit the ground running, who have the skills, experience, and confidence to work autonomously. In most cases, the FBI is a second career for individuals hired for the special agent position.

During my time in the FBI, physical files were pulled and dropped off in the supervisor's office for his or her review. Whether or not this was a back breaking task with a heavy load of main and multiple sub-files depended on the size of your caseload. Agents could be assigned to one major investigation or thirty cases in various states of active and pending status. Nowadays, it's all computerized. After the files are examined, the supervisor goes over each case to provide an assessment, and if applicable suggests investigative tools and techniques for the agent to consider exploring next. Accomplishments, such as how many interviews, searches, arrests, indictments, trials, and convictions have been logged in since the last file review, are maintained on an FBI form FD-515 (Accomplishment Report Form) informally known as a stat sheet. It's a highly visual way to determine if an agent is pulling their weight. Incentive awards (yearly bonuses) and merit pay increases are based on these recorded accomplishments. Squad members are often watching to see who has the bigger cases and the most stats—valuable bragging rights. The FBI can be a competitive environment. No one wants to be known as an empty suit.

On a task force or organized crime squad, several agents may be assigned as case agents to focus on the major players targeted in the investigation and the other members given the task of opening files on minor players and spin-off cases. Local and state law enforcement officers on the taskforce or squad are partnered with agents who, for the most part, assume the administrative responsibilities for their portion of the investigation and assess the work their partners produce. For example, the agent would be the affiant on a search or arrest warrant filed in federal court. Conversely, the advantages of a task force include the ability for the local law enforcement officer to obtain a state warrant if the investigation requires.

The primary objective of FBI special agents, no matter what squad or violation they are assigned to investigate, is to collect and assess intelligence. That's because the FBI is not just a law enforcement agency. It's also an intelligence-driven agency. Every field agent is evaluated on his or her participation in the collection of human intelligence (HUMINT), and everyone they speak with is considered a potential source. Gathering human intelligence is a mandated requirement and documented meticulously. Agents are evaluated on the number and quality of their key sources, also referred to as *symbolled sources, informants, cooperating witnesses,* and *assets.* The ability to communicate with people who are able to provide direct knowledge of criminal activity is one of the most important roles of an investigator.

From the FBI website

"Frequently Asked Questions"
What is the FBI's policy on the use of informants?

Although it is legally permissible for the FBI to use informants in its investigations, special care is taken to carefully evaluate and closely supervise their use, so the rights of individuals under investigation are not infringed. The FBI can only use informants consistent with specific guidelines issued by the attorney general that control the use of informants.

(https://www.fbi.gov/about/faqs/what-is-the-fbis-policy-on-the-use-of-informants)

Here's what retired agents I've interviewed have said about the development and handling of sources.

Retired agent Judy Tyler, in episode 004, "Drug Cases and Informant Development," spoke about why informant development is important to the FBI:

Judy Tyler (JT): Since retiring from the Bureau, I've been working as a contractor, providing instruction to agents on developing and operating informants at the FBI Academy or another location in Virginia. I can't really talk about a lot of it, but part of [the training] is done through role-playing, which is a great way to teach. It's better that the students make mistakes in dealing with me than the public. They interview me and try and figure out my motivations (to cooperate or not cooperate) and things like that, and I can teach in roles so that they get it.

And it's a great way to teach. I don't know if the listeners understand that developing informants or human intelligence sources is key to the FBI because that's one of the many tools that we use to gather information to gather intelligence. I would say [developing sources] is the cornerstone of every case in the FBI. Every single case is made with information from the public, and that's probably the most important skill to have—to be able to work with people.

Jerri Williams (JW): I know it was when I retired, and I retired about seven -eight years ago. Every agent was required and expected to develop informants. I take it that's still the case.

JT: Yes, that hasn't changed. It's really the bread and butter of our jobs. Any case that is a success has informants as a component to it.

JW: And I would imagine that the reason you were hired for this job is because, during your years working drug investigations, that was very important to your day-to-day existence and success—developing informants, getting these drug dealers and their associates to talk to you.

JT: It was probably one of the most enjoyable aspects of the job, truthfully, working with the people in the public, whether they were drug dealers or not, to put together a case.

———

Most agents would agree that sources are of value to investigations and should be treated as such.

Retired agent Dave Nadolski in episode 130, "Loomis Fargo Vault Sting, Informants," talked about the necessity of trusting and respecting the investigative contributions made by informants:

Dave Nadolski: You see on TV that a guy's a snitch, that's what they call him. They portray him as a sniveling drug addict, and he'll walk up and dime somebody out for five bucks. [The public] is watching this and saying, "This guy is nothing but a rat. He's a rat." That is not the way to talk about an informant. That's not a way to treat an informant. That's not my experience. If you want somebody to help you, somebody who is on the inside because we're all on the outside, you've got to be genuine with him. You've got to protect him to [encourage] him to want to do it.

You also have to be selective [about] who you use. There were informants I used who have burned me and I was taken advantage of. But it didn't happen in this case and this turned out to be the biggest case of my life. And Tony did not regret doing it. He did not regret doing it. He was proud of it, I'm happy to say. Informants are people who have done things different than us, not necessarily approved by us. But if we want to get something done, we've got to travel in their shoes, we have to operate in their world. We can't do that without them. They are invaluable.

FBI Film and Fiction Review

American Hustle

This 2013 black comedy and crime drama was inspired by the FBI ABSCAM operation of the late 1970s and early 1980s. I saw the movie several years ago when it was first released. I watched it again recently, and this time I took notes on the clichés and misconceptions about the FBI. The movie follows a fictionalized version of the actual ABSCAM investigation. Bradley Cooper plays Richie, a young FBI agent investigating a con man operating an advance-fee scheme. Christian Bale plays the part of the con man. The methods and technical equipment used to gather electronic evidence were accurately depicted. However, the film uses creative license when it comes to the romance between FBI agent Richie and his cooperating witness "Lady Edith" (played by Amy Adams) and his physical assault of his supervisor. These are fireable offenses. In the Bureau, there are many prohibitive behaviors, and an inappropriate sexual relationship with an informant or cooperating witness is one of them. Insubordination is another, and assaulting a supervisor or any other employee would not be tolerated. The egregious actions displayed during the telephone beating scene were so over-the-top that I was distracted for the remainder of the movie. In the movie, Richie and his supervisor also pointed guns at each other. In what workplace would that be acceptable? The movie also stars Jennifer Lawrence and Jeremy Renner. **Spoiler Alert:** At the end of the movie, Ritchie is fired for misplacing $2 million (this did not happen in the actual case), which is his third strike. In real life, an agent would most likely be investigated and criminally charged for such an offense.

My rating for *American Hustle*: Has anyone seen my shoe?

Retired agent Myron Fuller in episode 052, "The Original ABSCAM, Con Men and Mob Guys," spoke about how his cooperating witness, Mel Weinberg, was the inspiration for actor Christian Bale's character in the movie American Hustle:

Jerri Williams (JW): Most people associate ABSCAM with a movie that came out just a few years back and that's *American Hustle*. [How much was portrayed correctly in that film?] I understand that you were consulted [and that] you actually sat down with Christian Bale. Can you tell us about that?

Myron Fuller (MF): I spent a whole weekend with Christian Bale in his home in Beverly Hills, and Mel was there too. My purpose [for being there was two-fold]: keep Mel on track and also provide background information for the parts of the movie that were real [such as how we really conducted our banking at

Chase Manhattan Bank]. When Mel came forward to offer his cooperation, it was motivated by two things: to keep his girlfriend out of jail. He was married but he also had a mistress, so that part of the story was also kind of similar to what they showed in the movie. [Two,] he also wanted to keep himself out of jail. That was his motivation to cooperate.

———

But there are times when an agent's reliance on a source may back fire and cause potential damage to the case and the agent's career.

FBI Film and Fiction Review

The Informant and The Informant!

The true crime book by Kurt Eichenwald, published in 2000, is a compelling story of power and betrayal that was also made into a feature film in 2009 with Matt Damon in the title role. The FBI case was an anti-trust corporate fraud investigation involving Archer Daniels Midland ADM, a global food processing company operating a price-fixing scheme to steal millions of dollars from its customers. The case was code-named Operation Harvest King. Mark Whitacre, senior executive with ADM, one of America's most politically powerful corporations, became a confidential government witness. However,

Brian Shepard and Bob Herndon, the FBI agents assigned to the investigation learned during the case that their informant was not telling them the whole truth. In the movie version, they can't be certain where the lies stopped, and the truth began. Their rogue cooperating witness had a hidden agenda that nearly destroyed the careers of Herndon and Shepard, played by actors Joel McHale and Scott Bakula respectively in the film.

The Informant is my favorite narrative nonfiction book. It reads like a cleverly conceived novel. The fact that it is all true is a bonus. The way author Kurt Eichenwald crafted the story inspired me to write crime fiction, where the story is about the characters more than the crime. I must admit that I had to watch the movie a second time before I embraced its dark satire.

My rating scale for *The Informant*: No footwear was removed while reading this book, all laces were tightly bound. However, while watching *The Informant!*, I loosened the laces just in case.

Retired agent Bob Herndon in episodes 148 and 149, "The Informant, Price Fixing Case, Book, Movie," spoke about what it was like to have a book and a movie produced about his case:

Bob Herndon (BH): There's a lot that went on in this case. The author told me that the book was originally about fourteen hundred pages, so he had to cut out a lot. Nothing is perfect. The book's not perfect. The movie is not perfect, but what a real testament to people to try to tell a story. I'm glad you enjoyed it.

Jerri Williams (JW): Definitely. Is there anything that was in the book or shown in the movie that did not occur or that you want to comment about?

BH: There are things left out of the book, but that's just because it would be too long. I know in the movie there's a scene toward the end of me talking to Mark in prison. Brian's off the case or doesn't want to have anything to do with Mark. Mark's already been sentenced, the price-fixing case was over, and I'm helping Mark with his pardon, according to the movie, and meeting him in prison. In the scene, Mark lets it slip out that he might have taken $11 million.

JW: Yeah, $11 million. So that didn't happened?

BH: No. I never met him in the prison. But let me say this: Mark did keep changing the amount of the fraud. It was always changing. Even up to right before he went to prison, the amount of the fraud was changing. So that idea that the dollar amount kept changing is correct. Going past $9.5 million was just to create mystery for the movie audience, indicating that $2.5 million was still hidden someplace.

JW: It worked.

BH: Yes, it worked. And I did not work with Mark on his pardon in prison.

#6 *AGENTS ARE UNEMOTIONAL AND HAVE NO SENSE OF HUMOR*

Beyond the Caricature

The strait-laced, no-nonsense image of an FBI agent is a holdover from the days of former FBI Director Hoover, when agents could be fired or banished to Butte, Montana, for minor infractions such as wearing the wrong color shirt (i.e., anything other than white). There's a story about a young agent at FBI Headquarters who found himself stuck on the same elevator as Director Hoover. They did not exchange a single word, but later that day, the young agent was told he had been fired. His infraction? Acne. Director Hoover believed that the agent and his blemished and pocked complexion did not represent the FBI well.

Consequently, agents were careful to comport themselves with behavior and appearance beyond reproach. This has become a caricature, creating the mechanical, unemotional body in a suit that has been seen and described in many films and books about the FBI.

FBI Retired Case File Review listeners know this image is false. Agents care deeply about the people they work with, the victims and the subjects of their investigations. One of the things that listeners say surprises them the most is how much the agents are emotionally tied to their cases, how much the work and the people involved mean to them. The opportunity to hear and learn about FBI agents' thoughts, feelings, and perceptions as they attempt to solve their complex investigations provides the public with an intimate view of law enforcement they never had before.

In episodes 126 and 127, "Yosemite Park Murders, Child Predators, PTSD," retired agent Jeff Rinek spoke about showing compassion when working with violent crime victims and suspects:

Jerri Williams (JW): I just want to make sure you explain what you mean by showing compassion and making the subject, no matter how bad they are, think that you understand, that you know what they're going through, that it wasn't their fault.

Jeff Rinek (JR): Exactly. And for me, it's not an interview tactic. I interviewed a kid one time and in the lead up to getting him to talk about the crime and trying to get to know him, I said to him. "If you could have anything in the world, what would you want?" His answer was, "I would want someone to love me and I would want to have someone to love." How does that not affect you? That told me that this kid, who had committed a murder, had other things going in his life. He might have had some mental illness issues, but it also told me that he wanted to have someone, he wanted to be with someone. So I don't judge. It's not cut-and-dried. It's not like it is on TV, when you conduct one of these interviews and then go home and play ball with your kids. It's not like that for me.

I was being interviewed for a TV show and I told them not to ask me if this case was more important to me than the others. And sure enough, they asked the one question I told them not to ask me. My answer was: How can you tell one victim's family that a different victim means more to you? All these cases were as important to me, and for each one of them, when I came home, I shared the effect they had on me with my wife.

———

The level of emotional engagement discussed in this excerpt shows how seriously agents are invested in their work and that they are not cold or unemotional. And there's also a lighter side to interactions among agents. Perhaps a little joking around serves as a comic relief for the difficult situations witnessed.

Practical Jokes

Every day in the FBI has the possibility of being different than the one before. What you're going to be asked to do can be unpredictable. You might be expecting to come into the office one morning to handle paperwork, and the next thing you know, you are heading out on an arrest or to execute an emergency search warrant. The FBI has a culture of camaraderie because the agents must depend on each other in order to accomplish their jobs. Because of the long hours worked and the often-dangerous missions, squad members develop close personal relationships where friendly teasing takes place regularly. Many of the stories told during podcast interviews illustrate that FBI agents take their jobs seriously, but not necessarily themselves.

Agents are assigned to squads based on related violations. Each squad is like a large dysfunctional family. When appropriate, there are lots of laughs and jokes. Just like mischievous siblings, squad members have been known to pull practical jokes on each other. A common prank is when an agent leaves their credentials out on their desk and their official ID photo is covered with a photo of a cartoon character such as Mickey Mouse or Homer Simpson. Unfortunately for the agent, they usually don't know their credentials have been tampered with until the next time they take out their badge to display to an interviewee. The result is an amusing, albeit embarrassing, situation.

Careful though, jokes can back-fire. After reading an email advertising an upcoming firearms shoot being held exclusively for female agents, I remember one agent in the Philadelphia Division sending back a Reply All message asking, "Is there a limit? How many female agents can we shoot?" Let's just say his joke didn't go over very well.

Nevertheless, there's a lot of hilarious stories that are legendary throughout the Bureau and shared among the rank and file. I'm sorry that I can't share many of them with you here. Just take my word on it—they are too funny. With a few exceptions, it's all good clean fun.

In episode 015, "Toddler Kidnapped for Ransom and Ira Einhorn," retired agent Mike Carbonell talked about the practical jokes played by agents on his violent crimes and fugitives squad:

Mike Carbonell: We put the case on the TV show *America's Most Wanted*. Ritchie, my partner from the DA's office, and I went down to the television studio in Washington, D.C., on the night the show aired, to monitor the tip calls as they came in. We knew Einhorn was in Europe, and we were hoping someone in Europe would call us. He looks like a biker, so everybody who knew a biker in America ended up calling to say that he was living in Arkansas or Southern California or whatever. At the end of the night, I have all of these tip sheets I'm going through, and one of them says the fugitive was sighted in this town in New Jersey, which is where I live.

I said, "Rich, look at this. Here's a tip from South Jersey." Then I said, "Oh wait a minute. What the heck?" The sheet said Einhorn was living on this road in this town in New Jersey. It gave my address and said the fugitive was a little bald guy with bad breath. I quickly figured out that one of my squad mates called into *America's Most Wanted* and gave them my address. I howled. I knew who did it.

FBI Film and Fiction Review

Whiskey Cavalier

When it comes to FBI agents taking their jobs seriously but not necessarily themselves, the ABC series *Whiskey Cavalier* (2019) illustrates that premise well. The charming spy drama follows the adventures of FBI agent Will Chase (actor Scott Foley), code-named Whiskey Cavalier, and kickass CIA officer Francesca "Frankie" Trowbridge (played by actress Lauren Cohan). Will is forced to partner with Frankie on international investigations of interest to both the FBI and CIA, but their relationship is complicated. Following an emotional breakup, Will's sensitive side is raw and exposed, and Frankie doesn't hesitate to take advantage of his vulnerabilities to keep the upper hand in the partnership. Together, they lead an interagency team of quirky spies who manipulate, play tricks on, and laugh at each other as they tackle their dangerous assignments and kill a few bad guys along the way. I thought *Whiskey Cavalier* was funny and clever. Unfortunately, the action comedy was cancelled after only one season. (The show was loosely inspired by retired agent Eugene Casey and the time he served as an assistant legal attaché (ALAT) in the FBI Paris Office. Casey was a technical adviser for the show.)

The humorous antics and sticky predicaments make for a refreshing and not-so-serious look at the FBI. It's all fictitious and nearly devoid of factual procedures and protocols of the real FBI—but so was *X-Files* and I enjoyed that show too.

My rating for *Whiskey Cavalier*: I kept my shoes on my feet, but during the show, I loosened the laces just in case.

#7 *UNDERCOVER AGENTS RUN THEIR CASES*

Going Undercover

A case needs a case agent. Although undercover agents (UCAs) play a vital role, the case agent is in charge of the investigation and the undercover agent and the case agent are seldom the same person.

That's not to say that a case agent can't pick up the phone and pretend she is someone else or, during an initial meeting, introduce herself using a fictitious identity. However, a significant undercover role is not played by the agent assigned to investigate the case. Instead, another agent is selected and approved to assume that part of the investigation.

The use of a UCA is considered only after other covert investigative methods and tools—such as the use of informants, consensual monitoring, and electronic surveillance—have been explored. Before an undercover agent can be introduced into an investigation, authorization from FBI Headquarters (FBIHQ) must be obtained. The case agent prepares a Group I or II undercover proposal that is first submitted for preliminary approval to the SAC of the division, with the concurrence of the U.S. Attorney's Office. The proposal outlines the predication that initiated the opening of the case and the anticipated outcome of the proposed undercover scenario. Once the undercover committee in the field approves, then it's sent up the chain for FBIHQ authorization.

Once approved, the case agent submits a list of the skills and attributes needed for the UCA role and the Undercover Unit at FBIHQ provides the names of experienced UCAs available. The case agent interviews the potential UCAs about the assignment and selects the agent determined to be the best fit. It might help to look at the case agent as the casting agent, producer, and director of the investigation and the UCA as the actor playing a role. The case agent provides a script to the UCA, outlining the objective of the undercover scenario. Are they seeking to buy drugs, record incriminating statements, or perhaps identify additional targets? Of course, the UCA can improvise and alter the script as appropriate. The case agent handles everything behind the scenes that makes it possible for the UCA to do his or her job. At the same time, the case agent is juggling all the other aspects of the investigation, such as documenting surveillances, wire taps, and contacts with witnesses and subjects, as well as, maintaining expense reports.

"All that administrative B.S. that Dan was dealing with, I never knew anything about it. That's what a good case agent does."

—Retired agent Ray Marrow, episodes 138 and 139, "Cleveland Police Corruption, Undercover Sting"

One of the most important aspects of the case agent's responsibilities is reporting the status and results of recordings to the federal judge overseeing the warrants and court orders issued for the case.

Retired agent Mike McGowan, in episode 143, "Ghost, Working Undercover," talked about how undercover agents are portrayed in books and movies:

Mike McGowan: Truthfully, I have never been a big watcher of FBI stories because that's what you and I did every day of our lives. When I came home from work, I wanted to watch something else or do something else. When I see undercover agents portrayed, especially FBI or federal level undercover agents, they're almost always off the reservation, doing crazy stuff against policy and procedure. Nothing could be further from the truth. When you work undercover operations within the FBI, you have a very strict series of guidelines you have to follow— legal, procedural, and policy-wise. You just don't walk into a room and do whatever you want. There is a very clear, objective practice that we go through, so when we do present the case in court, the evidence will withstand defense scrutiny. So we're very careful how we setup and execute undercover operations. There's a tremendous amount of oversight. There's a tremendous amount of preparation. So to have FBI undercover operations viewed as just some crazy guy going off the reservation just isn't accurate.

Evaluation and Training

Being an undercover agent is a voluntary assignment, but not everyone who raises their hand is chosen. Intensive training and role-playing seminars determine an agent's suitability, especially for those going deep undercover with no badge and no gun.

An additional agent working on the case agent's squad and familiar with the investigation may serve as the UCA's contact agent. The FBI understands how crucial it is for there to be a lifeline available to reach out to the UCA on a regular basis and monitor the UCA's mental fitness to continue the assignment. The contact agent meets with the UCA to check on their well-being and pick up evidence, such as audio and video recordings and the UCA's investigative reports. This agent is also responsible for relaying pertinent intelligence gathered using other investigative techniques to the UCA.

A UCA is required to undergo mental health evaluations before and during an assignment. They will return to Quantico every six months for an evaluation and stress test. Even so, undercover agents report that it is easy to start empathizing with their subjects and developing genuine concern and affection for the targets of the investigation. The isolation and loneliness experienced by FBI agents going undercover for long-term assignments is an occupational hazard beyond the risks of their true identity being detected. The public is fascinated by stories, true and fictional, about the exploits of UCAs.

Agents are required to have a few years of field time before returning to the academy for undercover training. Experienced UCAs are often asked to lecture and teach at the academy, so new UCAs may learn from their experiences.

Retired agent Barbara Verica in episode 018, "Undercover Spy and Investment Fraud," spoke about the isolation and loneliness she experienced during a two-year undercover assignment early in her FBI career, a time before an official undercover training program was established at the FBI Academy:

Barbara Verica (BV): It was a very difficult case from an emotional standpoint for me.

Jerri Williams (JW): Especially since you did not have the support of an undercover program because none existed at that time, right?

BV: That's right. I didn't even have much support from my own squad. I couldn't tell people what I was doing. The only people who really knew what I was doing were the people I worked with. Many times there were inherent difficulties when working undercover. For instance, I would tell them, "Here's what I said to her when she asked me this question," and they would mull it over and say, "You shouldn't have said that. You should have said this." Finally at one point, I said, "You have a luxury of sitting around and discussing what I should say and what I shouldn't say. I don't have that luxury. I have to give an answer instantaneously and you can't be telling me that's wrong. You're going to have to live with it." So we had a little bit of a problem there, and that was a tough one. I think the training for undercover agents is very important. Obviously, they found that out, and I think that's something that goes on now within the FBI.

JW: Yes. People are vetted before they are allowed into the program.

BV: Absolutely. And they should be. And anybody who's supporting that person should also go through the training as well. They need to understand what the person is going through when they're undercover. It's not easy.

JW: Well, it sounds like it was an emotional time for you. You made it through, but I can still feel, can still hear that it was hard for you.

BV: It was a difficult time, but the difficulty came with the fact that, for two years of my life, I felt I couldn't talk to anybody. My family didn't know what I was doing. I couldn't tell them about it and I couldn't tell any of the people I worked with about it. That made me feel very isolated. And I certainly didn't go on any dates during that time.

————

There is the risk of undercover agents becoming too invested in portraying themselves as someone else.

Retired agent Jesse Coleman in episode 019, "The Sicilian Mob and Undercover Drug Deals," spoke about the relationships developed with targets while working undercover:

Jesse Coleman (JC): After they were taken down, I was instructed by my superiors that I had to go talk to Eddie and explain to him who I really was: "Show him your credentials and tell him that you're really an FBI agent." I did that.

Jerri Williams (JW): Why did they want you to do that right then and there?

JC: It's a safety issue. First of all, you do not want them to think that you were just an informant. Your life is in much more danger if they think you're an informant than if they know that you're an agent.

JW: So they do have respect for law enforcement: "An informant, let's kill him. Let's get rid of him." But if they knew that you were actually law enforcement, FBI, then there's much less chance of that happening to you.

JC: Exactly. So I did that. He looked at me. He looked down, and he spit on my credentials. So, he was arrested.

JW: Hmmmm.

JC: Months later, we were going to trial. We're wondering, *Why are they going to trial? We have more than two hundred recorded conversations with them.* We couldn't figure out why. So I go on the stand and start to testify. I see the two guys looking at me. They stop the trial, and they plead guilty. Why? Because even at that point, they thought they were my friends. Our relationship had gone on so long that, even once they learned I was an FBI agent, they didn't believe I would actually testify against them. How did I feel? I felt depressed immediately after the arrest. It's a natural psychological reaction. I felt that I'd stabbed my friends in the back. Of course, shortly after, I realized that they're criminals. They weren't my friends.

JW: Wow.

JC: The undercover role, at times, becomes almost real to you. The person that you're pretending to be becomes almost real to you. I was really Jesse Carpenter, to a certain extent. I didn't have to go to the FBI office. I really had this luxury car, this money, this jewelry. But then I had to give it up. It was like, *Wow, I have to go back to the office like all the other guys and sit behind a desk every day.* You get over that, but that's something you really go through. Which is why I never did it again, undercover. Some guys, unfortunately that's all they can do after they been deep undercover for a long time. It's just a hard bond to break, to become a normal square again. But that's what I did.

———

If the role is played flawlessly, the bad guys will have no clue that the UCA isn't one of them.

Retired agent John Ligato in episode 021, "Mob Guys and Strip Clubs," talked about going undercover with Joe Pistone and how even organized crime figures were impressed by Joe's success in infiltrating the New York mob:

John Ligato (JL): Donnie Brasco was my partner. This is after he had come back in. He was my contact in Florida. It was kind of funny.

Jerri Williams (JW): This is Joe Pistone, Donnie Brasco from the movies.

JL: Yep. I brought two Cleveland wise-guys down there, and we took them out on the FBI undercover boat. We were having dinner after about the third day. We were discussing criminal activity. I think it was stolen cars. There's four of us at the table—there's me and Joe, I'm wearing a recorder, and Sam and Jimmy. The older made guy, Sam, says, "All right, we don't want to get infiltrated by the FBI." I look at Joe and I'm thinking, *There's four of us at the table. Two of us are FBI agents. You've already been infiltrated by 50 percent.*

JW: Now, that's funny.

JL: I'll never forget this. Sam looks at Joe and he says, "Can you read?" And Joe says, "Yeah I can read." Then Sam says, "Well, I'm reading this book, *Donnie Brasco.*" And he starts telling Donnie Brasco about Donnie Brasco, how he had infiltrated the Colombos and how you've got to watch out. Don't do this. Don't do that. I remember looking at Joe thinking,

We're burnt. But Joe sort of shook his head no. So at Christmas, Sam bought two copies of *Donnie Brasco*, wrapped them up as Christmas gifts, gave them to me, and said give one to your friend. I said, "Thanks, I'll do that."

JW: Are you serious? So when he first started talking about it, you thought it was like a subtle threat?

JL: Yeah. I thought he knew. What would you think?

JW: But he really was just very fascinated with the book.

JL: Yeah. You know what? Most mob guys watched that movie. They watch all those mob movies, and they critique them. But they watch every mob movie. I remember sitting down with those guys, and they wanted to watch mob movies, and they would say, "That would never happen. We don't talk like that. That's stupid." They would critique the shows. I always thought it was hilarious.

FBI Film and Fiction Review

Donnie Brasco

This *New York Times* bestselling true crime book, published in 1988, was written by real-life FBI undercover agent Joe Pistone. In 1997, the book was made into a major movie that was nominated for an Academy Award for Best Adapted Screenplay. Both the book and movie portray how, using the alias Donnie Brasco, Joe Pistone went undercover in New York for six years and infiltrated the Mafia. The movie, however, takes several liberties with the original story where, posing as jewel thief, Joe/Donnie provides information to his FBI colleagues on the inner workings of the New York mob and helps to identify significant power struggles within. In the feature film, the role of Donnie Brasco was played by actor Johnny Dep, actress Anne Heche played his wife, and Al Pacino starred as the low-level wise-guy who vouched for Brasco and paid the price.

My rating for *Donnie Brasco*: I kept my shoes on my feet, but during the movie, I loosened the laces just in case.

In episode 046, "Infiltrating the Mafia, Being Donnie Brasco," retired agent Joe Pistone spoke with me about what it was like to have a movie made about his life and the unflattering creative compromises made to his story:

Joe Pistone (JP): I always make sure I get this out when I do interviews. I never slapped my wife.

Jerri Williams (JW): I was going to ask you that. I figured that you'd want to get that out. That's at the very end of the movie. I thought, *If he wants to set anything straight I am sure he wants to set that straight.*

JP: Exactly. In fact, that was not in the original script. The director put that in on the day of shooting.

JW: Were you there?

JP: Yes, I was. When I found that out, I had some choice words for the director. We actually interrupted shooting for a few hours. But, unfortunately, the director's like the captain of a ship and what he says goes. I could not convince him that shouldn't be in there. So I lost that one. And also, I didn't have a bag with $300,000 in it.

JW: Yeah. Both of those things, as I was watching the movie, I was feeling for you, the character. And then when that happened, it was like, they dirtied it up. Why did they have to dirty him up?

JP: Well, yeah. It's the movies. So...

JW: Did you cut up a body?

JP: No, that's another thing. Actually, they did cut that gentleman up, but they cut him up with a chainsaw, not a hacksaw.

JW: You weren't there?

JP: No.

JW: Okay.

JP: Not just FBI but all law enforcement has really put a damper on [the Mafia]. I'm still involved. When I say I'm still involved, it's because I still do lectures and deal with police agencies. The mob is a criminal organization. That's it. All the resources aren't on the Mafia anymore. Law enforcement is more concerned about the Russians, the Albanians—these organizations—more than they're concerned with the American Mafia.

JW: Definitely it was romanticized. But you know the truth—you know it isn't as cool and romantic as they make it appear on TV. What do you think about *The Sopranos*? Did you ever watch that?

JP: Yeah, I watched a few episodes, and to me, *The Sopranos* showed how violent the mob is and the treachery within each group. The jealousy and the envy that takes place within these groups. Now, the boss going to a psychiatrist wouldn't have lasted too long in the real world. Everything else really showed the down-and-gritty lifestyle.

#8

THERE IS ONE CENTRAL DATABASE

Technology and Data Retrieval

It would be extremely productive if an FBI agent or analyst could type a few key words, tap Enter, and immediately receive back a complete profile on a person. Computers are great. Unfortunately, unlike what you see on many cop shows, it's impossible to gather everything ever known about a person from one central database. The National Computer Information Center (NCIC) is an electronic clearinghouse of crime data, but the records are only as up-to-date as the information regarding arrests, charges, convictions, and sentences entered by thousands of law enforcement agencies around the country. To obtain additional information, investigators need to access an endless number of additional on-line records, documents stored in local, state, and federal computer files. Court districts maintain their own records. The military has separate record-keeping systems. Medical and mental health records are not maintained as one resource. School records are stored in literally thousands of educational directories. Financial documents are indexed under the strict control of banks and credit-reporting companies. Most of the information contained in the above databases require a subpoena or search warrant to access it legally. Consequently, it could reasonably take an analyst weeks or months, not seconds and minutes, to gather a comprehensive file on a subject.

When it comes to making creative compromises when writing a book, script, or screenplay, accessing search engines to fill in a characters backstory is one of the tricks used to quickly move the storyline forward. As an author, I recognize the convenience provided by having an analyst report from her desktop everything an agent needs to know to move the action forward. However, when I see some of the data claimed to be accessible via a computer search, I have to shake my head and laugh out loud. I wish it were possible with a few keystrokes to suddenly have everything ever known about that person. A frequent scene on TV is one where an investigator in the field calls into the office and, within thirty seconds, receives a complete dossier on a subject based only on his license plate number. The elaborate details extracted from computer searches are always astounding. A list of a person's known enemies? A repository of a person's elementary or high school friends? A former soldier's military buddies and where they currently reside? A profile listing all of a subject's immediate family members and whether they're living or deceased? A prison inmate's prior cellmates in every facility he was in? Yep, all of these results have been received from data searches conducted during TV shows. Can you really get this type of drilled down info from a computer search in real life? No way, Jose. I watched one show where they were able to determine in less than a minute that someone was operating a marijuana growing operation by comparing the monthly increase in their electric bill from $150 to $600. Now, I'm not saying that an investigator couldn't obtain that information and come up with a similar conclusion. I'm saying that it can't happen from a few clicks on a computer. As is the case with all of the situations presented here, that type of information is obtainable, but through dogged investigative leg work, interviews, surveillances, subpoenas, and search warrants.

Most viewers understand that these are shortcuts inserted into a crime drama in order to save time. However, it can be assumed that there are individuals who, after watching these shows, believe that they have seen confirmation that Big Brother is indeed all-seeing and gathering information to add to the files they maintain on every person in the United States. Of course, this can't be further from the truth. Law enforcement is way too busy chasing bad guys to be concerned about law-abiding citizens.

From the FBI Website

"FBI 100: The Top Ten Myths in FBI History,"
Myth #2) The FBI has files on every American.

The FBI keeps investigative files on serious violations of federal law and major threats to our national security. We won't have a file on you unless you're a spy or terrorist or criminal or are suspected of being one (and we use the word *file* loosely, as we generally organize materials by cases, not individuals). Some people do appear in our files if they've provided us with information or were a victim in a case…or because an authorized third party requested information about them, but this kind of information is held under strict laws and for a legally specified period of time. Some people think that the FBI has a vast range of files on all the bad things they've ever done. Not true!

(https://archives.fbi.gov/archives/news/stories/2008/july/myths_072408)

Records Maintained by the FBI

The FBI does maintain files containing information related to investigations, finger-print records, and individuals charged with crimes. The purpose of maintaining these reporting systems is to equip the FBI, and their law enforcement, national security, and intelligence community partners, with the information they need to protect the United States while preserving individual rights. Although, the information gathered may be deemed confidential or sensitive, there are no secret files maintained on everyday Americans without criminal histories. The following are the types of records the FBI keeps.

Case Files — Documents gathered during an investigation are maintained in investigative case files, with sections for interview narratives (FD-302s) of witnesses, victims, and subjects; memos, communications, subpoenas, warrants, charging documents (affidavits, Indictments and Informations, etc.), photos, evidence and surveillance logs, transcripts of electronic recordings, and even newspaper articles. These files—many with multiple subfiles—are maintained as hard copies and digital records and are an accounting of the progress and results of work completed by the agents assigned to the investigation. The names and identities of all individuals and entities associated with the case are indexed for retrieval at a later date.

Fingerprint Files — Most fingerprints on file in the FBI's Integrated Automated Fingerprint Identification System (IAFIS) were voluntarily provided by individuals applying for jobs. The fingerprints on file were submitted as part of a pre-employment background check. Also on file are the fingerprints of people who have legally purchased firearms and, of course, fingerprints that belong to people who have been arrested. Upon request, local, state, and federal law enforcement agencies are able to access IAFIS and conduct automated fingerprint searches for matches to criminals and evidence.

Criminal History Files — The National Crime Information Center (NCIC) is a computerized index of criminal justice information, such as arrest records, warrants, adjudicated matters, criminal record history reports, as well as information on fugitives, stolen properties, and missing persons. It is available to federal, state, and local law enforcement and other criminal justice agencies and is operational twenty-four hours a day, 365 days a year. Authorized agencies can make an inquiry and receive prompt disclosure of information from the system in order to properly identify persons in custody, locate and return stolen items, apprehend fugitives, and notify police of missing persons.

FBI Film and Fiction Review

FBI

This CBS TV show (2018-) is produced by Dick Wolf, the executive producer of *Law & Order*. The series main characters are Special Agents Maggie Bell (played by actress Missy Peregrym) and Omar Adom

"OA" Zidan (played by Zeeko Zaki), who are assigned to the New York Division of the FBI. Maggie and OA do not appear to be assigned to any particular squad or have a squad supervisor and are therefore able to tackle a new and challenging investigation each week. During season one, they have chased down MS-13 gang members, white supremacists, human traffickers, drug dealers, armored car thieves, and people responsible for bombings, hate crimes, terrorism, serial murders, and kidnappings. They work directly for Assistant Special Agent in Charge Jubal Valentine (Jeremy Sisto) and Special Agent in Charge Dana Mosier (Sela Ward). A valuable contributor to the team is Analyst Kristen Chazal (Ebonee Noel) who is a wizard with computers and electronic devises.

From the moment I heard about the show, I hoped it would have an authentic, real-life feel, not just because of the highly successful gritty, ripped-from-the-headlines stories featured on *Law & Order*, but also due to the fact that, in 2016, Wolf's TV production team embedded a film crew inside the actual FBI's New York office to capture the behind-the-scenes stories of FBI agents and analysts at work.

However, creative license is used often in *FBI*. Will viewers be able to distinguish what's real and what's TV magic?

Regardless, *FBI* continues to be more than just another FBI action show by presenting the main characters with moral issues, in addition to basic policies and procedural dilemmas. Although not perfect, one of the best things about the show is the honest emotional connection the agents express for the subjects, victims, and witnesses involved in their investigations. That's an aspect of the FBI and its agents that is rarely shown on TV shows and movies.

My rating for *FBI*: I kept my shoes on my feet. But during the show, I loosened the laces just in case.

#9 AGENTS USE INTIMIDATION AND THREATS DURING INTERROGATIONS

Interview Techniques

There's always that scene in a crime drama where an FBI agent or police officer is interrogating a terrorist or violent gang member, and he's an inch away from the bad guy's face shouting and screaming threats in order to coerce him in to confessing. For most communications between agents and subjects, the appropriate FBI term is *interview*, not *interrogation*. And agents prefer to rely on their charm and skills of persuasion— definitely not force—to convince subjects and witnesses to cooperate. However, filming a scene where two agents say reassuring and sympathetic words to the hardened criminal sitting across from them, probably would be boring.

But think about it. The types of bargaining chips an agent has to offer up for information are better presented as beautifully wrapped gifts, as opposed to steaming bags of poop. These guys have seen it all and don't scare easily. Instead of threatening something the suspect doesn't want, say more time in prison, a skilled interviewer turns the narrative around and presents an offer of less time (or no time) in prison—something the suspect does want. It's all in the presentation. It's that old-honey-versus-vinegar-thing. Suspects are under no obligation to speak with or cooperate with agents. It's the FBI agent's job to convince them it's in their best interest to do so; the key is to figure out what they want and use that as leverage. Many successful plans to get a confession have been modeled from the wily ways of the 1970s TV detective Colombo, who presented himself as a friendly but clueless nice guy.

Plus, information obtained through intimidation and coercion is subject to being thrown out by a judge during a suppression hearing, where evidence is deemed inadmissible and excluded from being used during a trial.

"But the real question is: How do you motivate someone to cooperate in an interview like that. As an FBI agent the most important thing in any interview is building rapport and how you get someone to relax and open up and talk to you."

—Retired agent Eugene Casey, episode 095, "Terrorist Carlos the Jackal, Interview Strategies"

Another reason that adversarial confrontations are avoided is that, in addition to conducting interviews, agents are always looking to develop informants. Each encounter with someone who has access to information the FBI does not have access to is an opportunity to build rapport, to build an alliance with valuable and knowledgeable sources in the criminal world. That's why the bad-cop-versus-good-cop scenario seems to work so well in TV encounters. The subject rejects the nasty attitude of the bad cop but is attracted to the more respectful and positive mannerisms of the good cop. But real law enforcement officers know that the bad cop role is not necessary. Being the good cop means showing compassion and empathy toward the subject or witness, even if you have to fake it. However, those initial interviews can develop in to a quasi-friendship and mentoring relationship. The positive changes made by an informant of mine in a mortgage fraud case were recognized in an article in the *Philadelphia Inquirer* (using an alias, of course). Over the course of the two-year investigation on which he had assisted me and my co-case agent, he had morphed from a Camden, New Jersey, street thug, drug dealer, and deadbeat dad in to an employed, PTA-attending, single father of two. I used to keep a photo of his kids on my desk. I'm quoted in the article: "We're just so proud of his complete transformation."

Obtaining a confession is the primary purpose of interviewing a subject in custody. However, the secondary goal is to obtain their cooperation or flip them. Be nice to the person you speak with today, and he may become your informant or cooperating witness tomorrow.

"I always say that three things solve cases; witnesses, physical evidence, and confessions. We need witnesses, but they can inherently be unreliable. They only see part of what happens, and they can only remember part of that. By the time you interview them, they're not always sure. Physical evidence is good. It can be very subtle, and it can be very obvious. It can measure in things that are not present. And then there's a confession. That's a skill, learning how to talk to people, getting them to tell you their deepest darkest secrets."

—Retired agent Dan Craft in episode 132, "Jeffrey Dahmer, Interrogating Serial Killers"

In most crime dramas, there's a point in the story when a symbolic or, sometimes, a literal time bomb starts ticking; if A doesn't happen soon, then B will happen. B is usually a very bad thing. Often that time bomb centers on the interrogation scene. For instance, if the agent doesn't get the kidnapper to confess and tell her where the victim is, the victim will die. It's an important part of the story's complications and crisis. But in real life, for most interviews, there is no time crunch or time requirement. Investigators may take their time to develop a rapport, which may lead to the subject cooperating and pleading guilty, perhaps even testifying against associates or higher-ups in the conspiracy.

Being respectful and empathetic toward subjects benefits investigative results in other settings as well. When a polygraph is administered, an agent may spend three hours or more observing the subject and seeing how they act under stress. That's invaluable. The polygrapher needs to help the person being tested to relax, so that they can establish a baseline for comparison. A suspect is never totally eliminated by a non-deceptive polygraph result, but it helps the investigator to reduce the subject's priority and significance for the investigation. This same method is also used in crisis negotiations, to stall for time and calm things down. Most negotiators on TV negotiate for about a minute. It is easy to understand why though; since the TV show format demands that matters be wrapped up quickly, it's impossible to film a scene with prolonged and productive talks, during which rapport with subjects is established, additional intelligence is gathered, and operational plans are updated.

By the way, the FBI now records custodial interviews and agents can request authorization to covertly record non-custodial interviews. When I was in the FBI, most interviews, adversarial or otherwise, were not recorded or videotaped. Agents have always been required to take copious notes during interviews and then provide a written narrative recorded as an FD-302 report of interview.

In episode 040, "Hunting Fugitives, Wrongful Convictions," retired agent Bob Cromwell talked about the methods he used to convince Jeff Holt, a violent fugitive he had arrested, to confess:

Bob Cromwell (BC): Well, the idea when you get somebody in custody is to take advantage of the fact that you're the first one to talk to him. If a guy gets in jail, normally the jail-house lawyers will advise him immediately not to say anything. So when you take a person into custody, the first time you grab him is the time to try to get him to speak. So we took Jeff back to the office in Houston. A young agent came along with me on the ride. He sat down with me and Jeff, and we basically had a conversation. I'm a real believer in interviews being very similar to car sales pitches. You develop rapport with the customer, minimize the purchase price, rationalize it. Well, in talking to somebody who's done something terrible, you develop rapport, you minimize what they've been accused of, which is kind of tough sometimes when you're talking about really violent crime, but you still do it, then you rationalize. Then you close the sale. In car sales, that means getting the person to buy. When interviewing a felon, it's getting him to talk.

It was interesting. We're talking about football and basketball. We're even talking about bartending, which I don't know anything about. I asked the young agent with us to go grab Jeff a Pepsi, and he did. When he came back, he asked me if he could see me out in the hallway. I went out in the hallway, and the young agent said he couldn't understand why I was being nice to this guy. He couldn't stand to be in the same room with him. I told him, "We'll talk about this later." We're trying to come to an understanding of what this guy is capable of and what he did. We went back inside and basically I convinced Jeff that I knew he was guilty and that I was just looking for an explanation. I told him that he seemed like a decent person and there must be a logical explanation for why he had committed the crime. Finally, without too much hesitation, he stated that he had a drug problem and he had been high. He remembered seeing this attractive woman in her house and he remembered going through a window, but the rest of it was lost to him. He didn't remember anything else. That's a confession.

That's really all we needed at that point in time. I told the young agent afterward that we may have just prevented the victim from having to go through a trial, which for her would have been like going through an assault again. As it turned out, partly because of the confession, he went to court and pled guilty. He's still in prison, still a guest of the California Department of Corrections.

Jerri Williams (JW): It's really interesting how you explain your investigative method, because so many times on TV and in movies they show it as an adversarial interview, very aggressive. You might have a [good cop-bad cop situation], where one of them is being nice. But everybody in the room, in this particular case, was really trying to put Holt at ease.

BC: That's ideal. In my opinion, in my experience, you get a lot more by taking the route of developing rapport, minimizing, and rationalizing. Lots of times people want to talk to you if you just listen to them.

JW: Yeah. I agree. I use the same method.

BC: I've met a couple of fugitives that were actually really decent human beings. I don't include people who commit rapes and murders in that category.

FBI Film and Fiction Review

The Firm

The Firm, a *New York Times* bestselling novel written by John Grisham in 1991, was made into a movie (1993) of the same name starring Tom Cruise. This crime thriller follows protagonist Mitch McDeere, a highly sought-after recent law school graduate. Instead of going with one of the top New York firms, Mitch accepts a position with a small law office in

Memphis, Tennessee. Bendini, Lambert and Locke offered the best perks, a pre-arranged mortgage, a lease on a luxury car, and to pay off his student loans. Shortly after he starts working, he learns his new firm's primary client is the Chicago mob and the FBI pays him a visit and asks for his cooperation. During an intense interrogation scene, they lean hard on Mitch. They tell him that other attorneys at the firm who tried to leave ended up dead. Mitch wants to break free from the criminal law partners, but he doesn't want to be under the thumb of the FBI either. Using the high-level law skills the firm hired him for, Mitch negotiates with the FBI. He'll assist them as a cooperating witness in exchange for the early release of his older brother from prison and a substantial sum of money.

When Mitch's life and the lives of those connected to him are threatened, he must come up with a plan to make sure his lawyer colleagues get what they deserve, the FBI gets what it wants, and he, his wife, and his brother get away with their lives and some cash to make it all worthwhile. In addition to Tom Cruise, *The Firm* stars Jeanne Tripplehorn, Gene Hackman, Hal Holbrook, Wilford Brimley, Ed Harris, Holly Hunter, David Strathairn and Gary Busey.

I've always enjoyed watching *The Firm*. I watched it again recently and realized I was probably biased because the central crime is based on a fraud. After many years working on an economic crime squad, I'm partial to white-collar cases. However, none of my cases involved murder and mayhem.

My rating for *The Firm*: I kept my shoes on, but I loosened the laces just in case.

FBI SENIOR EXECUTIVES ARE OUT IN THE FIELD

Management and Advancement

I'm always surprised when the main characters in many of the books I read and the TV shows and movies I watch have management-level FBI agents actively conducting investigations out in the field. For example, a fictional FBI director is supervising an investigation or the special agent in charge is attempting to convince a subject to confess. In real life, seldom does FBI management above the supervisor level go out in the field to participate in searches or arrests. They had their time in the field, but once they've moved up the management ladder, their role is to secure the resources and relationships FBI employees, agents and support staff, need to accomplish their work. The last place the Director of the FBI, an assistant director in charge (ADIC), a special agent in charge (SAC), or even an assistant special agent in charge (ASAC) wants to be is in the field. What if something goes terribly wrong?

I'm only half joking when I say that. In the FBI, the name of the game in moving up the ladder is plausible deniability. Agents often warn each other, "When upper management gets too involved, an agent has lost all control of his case." Little good can come from the big bosses being on-site. If the operation is successful, they can always take credit for the positive outcome back at the office or behind the podium at the likely-to-be-scheduled news conference. The exception would be major events and exercises, such as domestic terrorism standoff or a prison riot. A special agent in charge of a field office could be temporarily assigned as the on-site critical incident commander to oversee the operation.

Being a Bureau manager is, at times, a thankless job. In addition to having to relocate often, it's high pressure. The best supervisors devote their energy to ensuring that the agents on their squads have all the resources and support needed to work their cases. Others seem to make decisions based on how it impacts their careers. Those kind of managers are definitely not going out in the field.

To be fair, one of the reasons FBI management is not often present at arrests and searches is their full confidence in the abilities of the case agent and squad members. Most people would be surprised at the autonomy and complete responsibility that field agents have when it comes to managing their caseload. All possible scenarios concerning arrest and search are prepared and reviewed before warrants are executed. With input from their supervisors, case agents (who else knows the targets better?) design arrest plans that are reviewed and signed off on by senior management. I always get nostalgic when watching scenes in shows where agents are gathered just before a raid at a staging site in some parking lot near the home of their target. There is nothing like that feeling of anticipation and the buzz of adrenaline when you have on your *FBI* emblazoned raid jacket over your protective vest, weapon with extra ammo, and a game plan to execute. You don't know how much I miss that!

At the field office level, the FBI has a much flatter and more efficient organizational structure than most city police departments. At the lower level, there are the street agents working together on a squad, then there's the squad supervisor. An assistant special agent in charge (ASAC) manages several squads and squad supervisors, and the ASACs all report to a special agent in charge (SAC). The three largest of the fifty-six FBI field offices around the United States—Washington Field Office in D.C., the New York Division, and the Los Angeles Division—are each managed by an assistant director in charge (ADIC), who is assisted by SACs responsible for specific programs violations. The territory of each one of the fifty-six field offices covers part of a state, all of the state, or several states by way of satellite offices known as resident agencies (RAs). An RA is managed by a supervisory resident agent or a senior resident agent, depending its size. Many are staffed by only one or two agents who handle every violation under the FBI's jurisdiction. Talk about autonomy—their supervisors may be hours away.

The FBI Headquarters organizational chart is more layered. There are additional levels of bureaucracy, with supervisory special agents overseeing programs, not people, and unit chiefs, section chiefs, in addition to a confusing number of deputy, assistant, and associate directors. There is, however, only one director of the FBI. Although the FBI follows some para-militaristic rules, foremost the need to respect the chain of command, agents in the field are able to meet with senior management on a relaxed first name basis. No need to salute and stand at attention until addressed. Most recent FBI directors make it a priority to visit each field office and shake hands with the troops, including retired agents. I'm proud to have photos with almost every director of the FBI appointed during and after my FBI career—Directors Sessions, Freeh, Mueller, Comey and Wray. The only exception is Director Webster, who led the Bureau when I first joined.

I've heard that during Director J. Edgar Hoover's tenure, meeting him was a risk. If he thought an agent's handshake was too weak or that you wore a disheveled suit that reflected poorly on the image of the FBI, you could be banished to a field office far away, like Butte, Montana. Recently, I heard a story about just how critical management used to be in Hoover's day. An agent received a memo to his file that he was due a merit pay increase, but it was being denied because of a misspelled word discovered in one of his written reports.

The fact that managers aren't able to be actively involved in investigating cases, and the frequent transfers between the field and FBI Headquarters, are some of the reasons many agents in the FBI have no desire to apply for supervisor positions. The special agent position is one job where people are fighting to stay at the bottom. I served for six months as the acting supervisor of the Cherry Hill Resident Agency out of the Philadelphia Division. It covered three counties in South Jersey. During this time, the division was preparing for an inspection of all administrative and investigative aspects of operations. I spent those months pulling data to put together the statistical charts and narrative interrogatories that highlighted the RA's accomplishments since the last inspection. I hated being stuck behind a desk. So, although, I had previously applied to be the supervisor of the economic crimes squad I had been on for eleven years, and was devastated (read: pissed off) when I wasn't selected, I quickly learned that not getting that job had been a blessing in disguise. Instead of applying for the open RA supervisor position, I took on the media representative and spokesperson role for the last five years of my career. That position proved to be one of the most influential and rewarding experiences of my time in the FBI.

In episode 121, "Watergate, FBI Public Perception Today," retired agent John Mindermann spoke about the status of FBI leadership when Director J. Edgar Hoover died:

John Mindermann (JM): Hoover, being such a dominant character for so long, left a tremendous void in his wake. I think we were really feeling that when this case came along.

Jerri Williams (JW): Can I make an observation? Of course, I wasn't with the FBI at that time. I didn't join the FBI until 1982. But from what I've read and heard, Hoover was such a leader that he made most of the decisions. Everyone around him was afraid to make decisions; they didn't know how to make decisions. They knew that if they got the chance to decide on something and they were wrong, they could jeopardize their job. So it sounds like once he died, there were all these so-called FBI leaders who did not know how to lead.

JM: That's absolutely the case. You very succinctly laid out what exactly the problem was. The problems that were faced and the way they were overcome in dealing with J. Edgar Hoover pointed to this whole area of dominant, singular, almost-obsessive control to the detriment of developing leadership underneath him to support his direction as the head of the organization, to have people prepared to fill in when he was absent or when he actually died on May 2. This ensured that the agents stayed in line, à la the Hoover mentality, I guess is the best way to put it. So Mark Felt had this very, very strong reputation, and there were others, the specific names of whom I'm not aware, but there was a general atmosphere of fear, rather than a healthy leadership style in the underlings who worked for Hoover. So these are the men who took over and were supposed to be driving the Bureau, but they really didn't have the experience.

———

Agents may blame their differences of opinion with management on the number of years their superiors have been away from the field. However, a supervisor may have valid administrative concerns that the agent has not considered.

Retired agent Gary Noesner, in episode 101, "Waco, Stalling For Time," spoke about how important it is for negotiators to have the support of management:

Jerri Williams: I found a passage (in your book)—a couple of sentences that I thought really highlighted some of these issues. You say, "Hostage negotiation is about managing yourself and the people around you." And then you go on to say, "That doesn't just mean the person on the phone. You also need to manage up, to make sure that your commanding officer is paying attention to what you're doing, supporting your decisions, and then fending off attempts to take actions that would undermine those negotiating decisions." I guess that's what you're explaining to us right now.

Gary Noesner: That's exactly what I'm explaining. Part of the problem lies in that many commanders in the FBI are historically—and I suppose even today—are more tactically oriented. You know, in law enforcement, we tend to be action-oriented folks. We see a problem and we solve a problem. If people don't comply with what we want them to do, we tend to want to use our force to make them do it. Negotiation is quite different; it's a more subtle and nuanced approach. Sometimes it's not fully appreciated. Going back to the information in my book that you just quoted, one of the big challenges for someone like me is not only dealing with the people on the other end of the phone who we're trying to get to surrender peacefully, but dealing with decision makers, to make sure they understand this is why we're doing it this way. That clearly was an issue and a problem we had at Waco.

FBI Film and Fiction Review

Manhunt: UNABOMBER

This 2017, eight-part television series loosely follows the FBI's investigation of Ted Kaczynski, who was known around the world as "the Unabomber." Although multiple agencies, including the FBI, ATF, the Postal Inspection Service, and numerous state and local police, worked to identify and apprehend the Unabomber for nearly seventeen years, the series covers the part of the investigation when investigators obtained and began to evaluate the infamous manifesto for clues. Through a number of flashback scenes, we are shown some of the incidents where sixteen bombs exploded throughout the United States, killing three and seriously maiming and injuring twenty-three victims. The series, following a fictionalized version of the real investigation, highlights the contributions of FBI Profiler Jim Fitzgerald (played by actor Sam Worthington) who battles dismissive bureaucratic FBI leaders who are wary of his pioneering use of forensic linguists to narrow in on Kaczynski's use of several quirky phrases that include; "eat your cake and have it too." Actor Paul Bettany plays Ted Kaczynski.

Because I was aware of the many creative compromises made with the true story, such as the use of a composite character to represent the work of case agent Max Noel, I wasn't able to fully emerge myself in the story. I interviewed Noel in episodes 056 and 057 of *FBI Retired Case File Review*.

My rating for *Manhunt: UNABOMBER*: I kept my shoes on my feet, but during the show, I loosened the laces just in case.

In episode 003, "Forensic Linguistics and the Unabomer," retired agent Jim Fitzgerald reviewed his career as an FBI profiler and his work on the Unabomber investigation. On another occasion, I spoke to him about the mini-series *Manhunt: Unabomber* and what it's like to have an actor play you in a TV show:

Jim Fitzgerald: I was in Atlanta, where they filmed everything. I was actually watching Sam (Worthington, the actor) sort of pretend to be me back in 1995, saying words that I told the writers I actually said back then in an office that looked just like a mid-90s bull pen—that's what we FBI agents call our desks and squad areas. The word I keep coming up with for this, I can't think of a better one, the whole process is surrealistic, dream like. I'm pinching myself saying, *That's really me on the screen.* It's not. It's an actor portraying me, but he's doing a pretty darn good job at it.

The Natalie character, who is my girlfriend now— she played no real role. There was another linguist, an older man by the name of Roger Shuy. He was a well-known forensic linguist and professor at Georgetown University. He's retired. At the time, I actually met with him and we went over the manifesto for a few hours—what were some of the words and language connections to it. Not being a linguist back then, I was very impressed with him. I told the screenwriter and director, and they both like this Roger Shuy character. But they spruced it up a little bit once they met the real Natalie, my real partner. They made up a character like her who was doing a post-doctorate at Stanford, which the real Natalie did but a few years later. So, that's creative license, dramatic license whatever you want to call it. What I'm telling everybody is my character, which was portrayed very well by Sam Worthington, is a composite character. While the language parts I basically own, anything the viewer sees about linguistics or language that was more or less me, as portrayed by Sam in the miniseries.

But there are some other parts where other agents did things, but they can't keep bringing in different actors to play different roles to portray all these things. So again, composite characters. Nonetheless, it's a story very well told about an agency which was really frustrated for seventeen years. The FBI just couldn't stop this case. They brought me in to help out as a profiler, and I wound up really kind of switching hats and putting on a linguistics hat or least a text analyst hat. Together we helped solve the case.

The real bosses were not clueless. They were very much hands-on. In my memoir, *A Journey to the Center of the Mind (Book 3),* Chapter 20 covers the Unabomber case. I describe the supervisors in the SAC, the ASAC, and some other agents I work with all very positively. We had some arguments and debates, but in the long run, we came together and wound up solving the case.

———

While some shows may deviate from the facts in order to enhance the dramatic value, others attempt to stay as close to reality as possible.

FBI Film and Fiction Review

Waco

This 2018, six-part TV series was based on the true story of the 1993 siege of religious leader David Koresh's Branch Davidian compound in Waco, Texas. It covers the fifty-one-day period in 1993, where a standoff between the FBI and the Branch Davidian's developed after ATF agents attempted to execute arrest and search warrants at the compound. A deadly gun battle ensued, resulting in the deaths of four ATF agents and six Branch Davidians. Many of the details about the actual siege and investigation were pulled from the book *Stalling for Time: My Life as an FBI Hostage Negotiator* by retired agent Gary Noesner and the biography of Branch Davidian survivor David Thibodeau. By using both books, the series, attempts to tell the story from the viewpoints of both sides of the conflict, which ends with the fiery death of seventy-six Branch Davidians. The FBI hostage negotiator character in the series, played by actor Michael Shannon, uses the name Gary Noesner, but the real Noesner told me the role is a composite of all the negotiators assigned to the siege. The series highlights the internal battles fought by the leaders of the FBI and the Branch Davidians, as each side sought to find a way to end the standoff. Actor Taylor Kitsch stars as David Koresh.

My rating for *Waco*: No footwear was removed during the viewing of this series, and all laces remained tightly bound.

Retired agent Gary Noesner in episode 101, "Waco, Stalling For Time," spoke about the use of composite characters and creative license during the making of the TV docuseries *Waco*:

Gary Noesner: They purchased my book rights. They also purchased the book rights to David Thibodeau's, one of the Davidians who survived the last day of the fire, book. Their goal was to have his book tell them what was going on inside and my book tell them what was going on outside. I thought that was a good approach to take, and it served well. I had input into all six scripts. Some of my recommendations they embraced and some they didn't for reasons of dramatic license and otherwise. I was on set on two occasions to watch some of the filming and was able to make suggestions to the actors and directors. Again, some of that was embraced and some of it was not for variety reasons. What you have is that I'm the only real FBI agent whose name they use in this series, mostly because of legal liability reasons. You also have some artificiality in any dramatized series. There's a consolidation of characters. In other words, the things that my character does were done, but not necessarily by me. They make other characters composite characters. In Waco, we probably had six or seven negotiators per shift. In the movie, there are just two, because they don't want to introduce the audience to six or seven different personalities.

There's a lot of this artificiality that you see, but the core story is what's really important. Having seen all six episodes, I think they've done a real good job. There were some issues that came up that I recommended as some editing tweaks and changes. I'm pleased. I'm sure there are people from the Bureau that were involved that will see it and see a ring of truth to it and legitimacy. There will be some that don't like it.

That's just the way it is. From the six episodes I've seen, I would challenge anybody to say what part of it didn't happen that they feel strongly about. I think the person today that knows only vaguely about Waco and never really knew what happened, is going to get a real education if they watch the series.

#11

FBI AGENTS WORK FOR FEDERAL PROSECUTORS

United States Attorney's Office

The FBI is its own entity. In some local municipalities, detectives are assigned to the district attorney's (DA) office and work under the direction of an assistant DA. But in the federal system, FBI agents work *with*, not *for*, prosecutors known as Assistant United States Attorneys (AUSA). Basically, the FBI investigates and the United States Attorney's Office (USAO) prosecutes. However, they consult often on the merits of a case and the status of the investigation.

When an agent initiates an investigation, he may consult the USAO for an opinion on the prosecutorial merits of a case, especially for complex matters. The FBI's job is to gather the facts and evidence, and present the results to the local US Attorney. Both agencies fall under the Department of Justice (DOJ). The USOA considers whether probable cause exists and if all the elements of the crime have been presented, before deciding to bring the case successfully to trial. There's no need to continue to gather information if the AUSA believes that it would prove to be too difficult to convince a jury to render a verdict of guilty. I had a case once where the corporation agreed to pay a $3 million fine for overcharging its customers, but none of the owners or officers were criminally charged with fraud. I wanted to take them to court, but the AUSA didn't believe the testimony of my cooperating witness would hold up under cross-examination.

Another misconception is that prosecutors go out in the field with agents to participate in investigations, searches, and arrests. With few exceptions, such as being present at an off-site command post to prepare contemporaneous warrants needed for a search or takedown, this doesn't happen. Usually, the AUSA is back at his or her office and available by phone to assist with obtaining the needed warrants and court orders. The majority of interviews are conducted by FBI agents, who then record their notes in FD-302 reports of interview, which are provided to the AUSA. Agents and prosecutors, do participate in some scheduled interviews together, especially proffers and witness preparations sessions.

Occasionally during the last stages of a case, the relationship between agents and the AUSA can become frustrating and even contentious. After months or years of investigation, when the case is nearing indictment the agent may believe that they have gathered all the necessary evidence to charge the subjects, but the prosecutor still wants more before they believe charges are ready to be filed. As this occurs, agents jokingly admit that they can start to sound like impatient children on a long car ride, as they conduct additional investigations and provide more evidence, repeatedly asking the AUSA, "Are we there yet?" When it's finally time to move on to the prosecutive stage, the AUSA uses all of the agent's work product accumulated in the case file, such as FD-302 Reports of Interviews; transcripts of recorded conversations; documents, physical, and forensic evidence; and surveillance memos and logs to prepare the charging document, either an information or indictment.

A criminal trial is where the investigators and prosecutors come together as a team. The AUSA is in charge of the court proceeding. However, because the case agent has been intimately involved in developing the facts and gathering the evidence presented in the information or indictment filed against the defendant, once the trial begins, the case agent is customarily seated next to the AUSA at the prosecutive table. Federal case law recognizes case agents as part of the legal team. After months and years of conducting interviews, reviewing records, comparing witness statements, logging transcripts of conversations picked up on wiretaps, and collecting and submitting forensic evidence for analysis, the agent has become the subject matter expert. It is acknowledged in case law that the prosecutor will require assistance from the investigator to keep it all together. The time just before a case goes to trial is called the "prep time," and it's where the agent works closely with the AUSA to organize the evidence and coordinate witness testimony.

This is why, in spite of the fact that they may be called to testify as summary witnesses later in the trial to clean things up or clarify evidence entered, seldom is the case agent sequestered. It is typical for witnesses to be denied access to court proceeding before their turn on the witness stand. In order to avoid their testimony from being shaped by what they hear or see in the courtroom or to ensure they don't conform their testimony to support the testimony of others, they are not allowed to sit in the courtroom and watch any of the court proceedings. Based on the valued and significant role of the case agent as a member of the prosecution team, an exception to this restriction is regularly made.

The TV show *Law & Order* illustrates the dichotomy between the investigation and the prosecution of a criminal act. The first third of the show features the police detective gathering the evidence. The second third of the show has the officers meeting with the assistant district attorneys to obtain subpoenas and warrants and prepare to charge the suspect. The last third of the show takes place in the courtroom, where the ADA presents the case to the jury. At the conclusion of each episode, the detectives and the prosecutors share the responsibility for the final verdict.

The trial is where the agent and prosecutor find resolution for their hard work. The ultimate pay off for all the long days and personal sacrifices made during the investigation comes when the jury foreman announces a verdict of guilty. The best is when the defendant, after reviewing the evidence against them, decides to enter a guilty plea and reject a trial all together. Of course, an acquittal can be devastating for all.

Agents and prosecutors who find that they work well together can become a formidable justice squad, choosing to team up over and over again. I certainly had my favorite AUSAs who were assigned to the Eastern District Pennsylvania United Sates Attorney's Office. These were the attorneys I really clicked with. That meant if I had a new case, I would call them up directly and give them a heads-up to ask that they be assigned the case, so we could continue working together. When preparing for and during a trial— which can last for weeks if not months—agents and prosecutors spend a lot of time together, working late evenings and weekends. The process is more bearable if they actually enjoy each other's company.

In episodes 138 and 139, "Cleveland Police Corruption, Undercover Sting," retired agents Dan Estrem and Ray Marrow spoke about the frustration of gathering additional evidence to support the prosecutor's desire for an airtight case:

Ray Marrow (RM): Before the third week, I get called to a meeting at my undercover apartment just before we go the next Friday night. Dan's there and Rick's there, as well as the two AUSAs. They do not like the fact that I'm not counting the money, and they do not like the fact that Bud is taking all the money and supposedly paying the cops.

Dan Estrem (DE): Let's give you a little background here for your imagination. You've got a huge room, and you have got police officers, some of them in uniform, standing guard on a door while you have a crowd of people gambling. They're inside the casino, so there's no way that they can claim lack of knowledge. I'm showing these tapes to the prosecutors, and they're still saying that's not enough. So you can imagine the conversations, and this is a family show, so I won't get into it [. . .]. But unfortunately, when they have to prosecute it, they have the final say. So Ray was given instructions that he's going to convey. Just keep in mind that police officers in uniform, standing inside of an illegal casino, guarding the door, checking people as they were coming in and leaving, was not sufficient for them to be charged with anything.

RM: In addition, throughout the night, I would pull the cops aside, put them in front of a camera, and just talk to them. "Hey, did you get your money? Is everything okay? Did you see anything?" And so we were getting that conversation as well. So I go to this meeting, and they tell me now I've got to count the money. I said, "Have you guys not listened to the other tapes? Bud won't let me count the money." They said, "You've got to count the money and you've got to do it with each police officer." So, naturally I'm upset. I'm really angry. But as usual, Dan calmed me down and said, look we'll figure it out.

———

When the case agent and the UCA have established a close relationship and they began working with an informant, the prosecutor may seem like the big mean critical parent in the threesome.

FBI Film and Fiction Review

The Wolf of Wall Street

No one knows for sure who nicknamed Jordan Belfort "the wolf of Wall Street." Many suspect that it was Belfort himself. Nevertheless, the moniker turned out to be a great title for the book he published in 2007, and the feature film, directed by Martin Scorsese and starring Leonardo DiCaprio, that followed in 2013.

The story covers the years when Belfort rose from a junior stock broker on Wall Street to the mastermind of the brokerage firm Stratton Oakmont, a securities scam based in Long Island, New York, where he and his associates defrauded investors of millions of dollars through fraud and stock manipulation. It's an unbelievable tale of temptation, corruption, and greed—the kind of FBI crime stories I love to read and write.

Jordan Belfort was eventually caught by FBI agent Patrick Denham, who was portrayed by Kyle Chandler in the movie. The Denham character was based on real life FBI agent Greg Coleman and I asked Coleman if there was any truth to the outrageous antics of Belfort and business associates portrayed in the movie. He said some of their real life actions involving sex and drugs were worse. After cooperating, Belfort served twenty-two months in prison for the securities scam and money laundering charges. The movie also starred Jonah Hill, Margot Robbie, and Job Bernthal.

My rating for *The Wolf of Wall Street*: I kept my shoes on my feet, but during the show, I loosened the laces just in case.

In episode 107, "Wolf of Wall Street, Jordan Belfort," retired agent Greg Coleman talked about the acrimonious relationship between the prosecutor and Belfort and the creative compromises made in the film:

Jerri Williams (JW): I read Jordan Belfort's book. First of all, in it, he said that you were too nice to be an FBI agent and he had a nickname for you: "Agent OCD." He hated the Assistant United States Attorney. He had a nickname for him too. But since this is a clean podcast, I can't say that name out loud. What was your relationship with Jordan Belfort?

Greg Coleman (GC): Let me address the prosecutors thing without going into name-calling. I understand that. You have to remember the prosecutor is the lightning rod here. Even though I'm doing all the work behind the scenes, the guy who is the bearer of the bad news is the prosecutor. And so when we came to Belfort and we gave him an ultimatum, a deal that he had to take and he had to take it within twenty-four hours or he'd be subject to the full prosecution, the prosecutor's the lightning rod for that. So I understand that the two of them did not get along. They did not like each other.

———

GC: I do wish the movie had tracked some other aspects of the case more closely. I would say overall, the movie is probably 70 percent accurate.

JW: What would you have liked to have seen done differently?

GC: I don't think they ever made clear the difference between the Securities and Exchange Commission and the FBI and the two investigations. The SEC was done with their case by 1994. What Belfort was ultimately charged with had nothing to do with the SEC's case, although their case was the genesis of ours. You have to acknowledge that. But the crimes that Belfort committed, most of them—certainly the international money laundering aspect of it—were not involved in the SEC case. They weren't involved in that. In the movie, there's a merging of civil and criminal SEC and FBI. I don't think they ever make that distinction clear at all. I think they merged the two together and it's never made clear.

The other aspect—for example, when we arrest Belfort, he pleads guilty and cooperates right away. However, in the movie, he's played by Leonardo DiCaprio, and he says, "Look I'm not going anywhere. You'll have to come get me out of here." It's a big rah-rah, cheering-type scene. But that actually isn't the way it worked. Belfort was actually much smarter than the character in the movie. He understood he's going to jail for twenty-one to twenty-seven years if he doesn't cooperate against other people. Whereas in the movie, he does the stand-up thing and doesn't cooperate. Same thing is true for Todd Garrett, whose name in the movie is Brad. In the movie, he's a stand-up guy. He goes to jail and doesn't rat anybody out. In reality, he cut a deal with us to get his wife a pass. He cooperated against Belfort and became a pretty good witness for us. He brought us some physical evidence, like deposit slips from the Swiss bank and things like that that we ultimately used against Belfort. I just think some of the events in the movie, if they had tracked them closer to real life, it actually could have been a better movie. But I understand they are in the business of making movies to make money.

THE CIA HUNTS SPIES
IN THE UNITED STATES

Espionage

When most people think about espionage they think about the Central Intelligence Agency (CIA). However, when it comes to averting threats to national security in the United States, the FBI is the lead agency. The Bureau's intel mandate is to safeguard the nation from theft of trade secrets and intellectual property, and political interference directed against our democracy and citizens. The distinction between the two agencies is important because, unlike the FBI, the CIA has no law enforcement authority. FBI agents conducting counter-intelligence investigations are able to utilize the Department of Justice criminal legal processes and individuals caught spying in the United States can be tried in court and sent to prison. The exception is if the persons accused of committing espionage are foreigners in the United States under diplomatic cover. In that case, the spies have diplomatic immunity and cannot be prosecuted. The only recourse is to expel them from the country—unless, of course, the FBI can recruit them and convince them to become double agents.

Let me step back for a moment and provide a basic understanding of the difference between working espionage as an FBI agent and as a CIA officer. That sometimes gets confusing for people. The main thing to understand is that the CIA's mission is to gather and analyze foreign intelligence, to collect information on the status of another country's economy and defense. It is the FBI's mission to prevent foreign governments from gathering and analyzing America's intelligence, especially when this activity impacts our safety. This is known as counter-intelligence work.

"CIA case officers, their job is to collect intelligence overseas from foreign countries—political information, economic information, military information, information on things like coal production, and whatever is going on in any particular country. That's their job in the CIA. The FBI has a counterintelligence function. We are to identify, penetrate, and neutralize the activities of a CIA-type person who is in this country as a foreign intelligence officer, like a Russian KGB officer, or a Chinese intelligence officer, or even an intelligence officer from a friendly country, say from France, perhaps. Our job is to defeat their efforts in trying to collect the United States' secrets. CIA officers

overseas collect foreign intelligence, foreign government secrets for our benefit, for the benefit of our fighters, and the president so he can stay on top of the world situation. The CIA are our spies overseas. It's the FBI who hunts the spies in this country."

—Retired agent John Whiteside, episode 009, "NSA Spy Espionage Case"

However, the CIA and the FBI work together as needed to protect common interests. An example of this collaboration was the two-year-long investigation where FBI and CIA personnel successfully identified CIA Officer Aldrich Ames as a KGB mole. Ames, who was directly responsible for the execution of several Soviet and Russian assets and operatives, was charged and convicted of espionage in 1994 and is serving a life sentence. We know about this case because Ames was prosecuted in criminal court. As a matter of fact, retired agent Dell Spry received the FBI Director's Award for Excellence in a Counterintelligence Investigation and the CIA Director's Meritorious Service Award for his efforts in the matter.

"Most of the time we cannot speak about the accomplishments that we've had because they're classified and will be classified long after we're gone. So, it's kind of a neat world to operate in and there's been so many heroes in that world that have been unrecognized. Those guys they have done such incredible things on behalf of the entire U.S. intelligence community and

they will never ever be able to talk about it. No one knows what these guys did. They can never tell people the incredible things they've done and the fact that they did it and the fact that no one knows, to me, makes them unsung heroes. That's exactly what they are."

—**Retired Agent Dell Spry, episode 037,**
"CIA Betrayal, Aldrich Ames"

From FBI website

"What We Investigate"
Counterintelligence

Spies might seem like a throwback to earlier days of world wars and cold wars, but they are more prolific than ever—and they are targeting our nation's most valuable secrets. The threat is not just the more traditional spies passing U.S. secrets to foreign governments, either to make money or advance their ideological agendas. It is also students and scientists and plenty of others stealing the valuable trade secrets of American universities and businesses—the ingenuity that drives our economy—and providing them to other countries. It is nefarious actors sending controlled technologies overseas that help build bombs and weapons of mass destruction. And because much of today's spying is accomplished by data theft from computer networks, espionage is quickly becoming cyber based.

(https://www.fbi.gov/investigate/counterintelligence)

I can attest to this veil of secrecy because my best friend and former college roommate also became an FBI agent. Early in her career, Carol Philip Sydnor was assigned to work counterintelligence matters in the Washington Field Office. Later in her career, she received the FBI Director's Award for Excellence in a Counterintelligence Investigation. I'm very proud of her accomplishments, but to this day I have no idea what she did to earn that distinguished recognition and probably never will. One thing I do know is the work of Carol and her CI teammates, no doubt, helped to protect the national security of the United States, because that was their mission.

The FBI agents working counter-espionage cases are not collecting information concerning the domestic activities of regular US citizens. Information is gathered only for those who are participating in the theft and release of information and documents from the US government or U.S. companies that is considered classified, sensitive, or proprietary. Americans have been caught in treasonous acts, selling their companies' secrets to our foreign adversaries. Men like FBI agent Robert Hanssen, CIA Officer Aldrich Ames, and Navy Officer John Walker provided information to the former Soviet Union, and their betrayals resulted in the deaths of unknown numbers of military soldiers and sources.

"When we heard the damage assessment, [it was] a real downer because the NSA guys said it was catastrophic and it made us feel kind of guilty. We were getting what we wanted. We were counter-intelligence people, and we were living for good cases, and this was a great case, really a great case. But it was also a loss to our country. It was such a damaging thing. We were glad in the end to be responsible for bringing it all to justice. It was a great case."

—Retired agent Joe Wolfinger, episode 079 "Family Espionage, John Walker Spy Ring"

FBI Film and Fiction Review

The Americans

The FX TV series *The Americans*, which ran for six seasons from 2013 through 2018, followed the complex marriage of two Russian KGB officers posing as Philip (played by actor Matthew Rhys) and Elizabeth Jennings (played by Keri Russell), a husband and wife with two kids living in the Washington, DC, suburbs of Virginia—a modern American family of spies. The show starts in the early 1980s, during the Cold War. Philip and Elizabeth were initially assigned their identities and their union arranged, but during the clandestine operation, their relationship develops into genuine love. As the stakes get higher and the likelihood increases that they could be discovered by the FBI, especially their special agent across-the-street neighbor Stan Beeman (Noah Emmerich), Philip and Elizabeth are torn between their KGB duties, their love for each other and their kids, and living the American dream. Every episode highlights the moral dilemma of masquerading as someone else and lying to everyone you know.

I binge watched the entire six seasons during a three-week period. I found the series to be an extraordinary peek inside the world of counterintelligence (CI). Yes, the show used dramatic license to increase the drama and action. Almost every show featured at least one brutal murder. I never worked CI during my career, but notwithstanding the recent accusations of Russians poisoning expatriates overseas, I want to believe that their spies living in the United States aren't killing Americans on a weekly basis and we aren't doing the same to them. The interactions between FBI employees, the look and feel of an FBI squad, the family sacrifices agents make, and their commitment to their mission were brilliantly showcased in each exciting episode. Plus, watching *The Americans* is like taking weekly mini courses on trade craft.

My rating for *The Americans*: No footwear was removed during the viewing of this series.

#13

THE FBI CAN WIRETAP ANYBODY, ANYTIME

Electronic Surveillance

Electronic surveillance, the recording and monitoring of individuals, conjures up images of government spying that makes US citizens uneasy. Is Big Brother out there watching and listening? Even the gag name "FBI surveillance van" some people use for their Wi-Fi username can have many people laughing uncomfortably. Most Americans don't think having their civil liberties and privacy violated is funny.

Almost every FBI TV show or movie has a scene where agents wearing headphones are sitting in a parked van listening to a conversation taking place in a nearby restaurant. In most instances, the fictional agents are monitoring a consensual interaction between two parties, the subject of an investigation and an informant or undercover agent (UCA). In addition to recording the discussion, the agents are listening to a transmitter relaying the audio in real time, so the safety of the source or UCA can be monitored. In this scenario, where one of the parties engaged in the conversation has given prior consent to the monitoring or recording, a warrant is not required. This guideline includes when the party providing consent is an FBI agent. The special agent in charge of a field division, with concurrence from the local United States Attorney's Office, can administratively approve consensual monitoring for non-telephonic body recorders and transmitting devices and telephonic consensual monitoring of a nonsensitive nature.

The recording methods noted are not what is commonly referred to as "wiretaps." A wiretap is the interception of wire, oral, or electronic communications where there is no third-party consent involved. It's when a bug is installed in the ceiling tiles of a union meeting hall where a business leader is being extorted or when a digital device is installed behind the radio panel in a luxury car where drug deals take place or in a lamp in a hotel room where a public official is accepting a bribe. However, to listen in on private conversations taking place outside of the presence of a cooperating source or UCA, the FBI must obtain authorization from a federal judge. The guidelines and protocols for the use of these sensitive electronic surveillance techniques are strictly defined under federal statutes, Title 18, U.S. Code, Section

2516. The application is made in writing and under oath. The agent or agents involved in the installation and monitoring of the wiretap could have the evidence obtained suppressed or, the worst scenario, be charged with a criminal violation if the proper protocols and rules of disclosure are not followed.

Before a federal judge will consider authorization of a wiretap, a detailed application must be submitted establishing the facts of the investigation and the underlying alleged felony offense, probable cause that a felony has occurred or will occur, and information supporting that the wiretap may provide additional evidence of the violation of federal law. The FBI agent seeking authorization must also provide a description of the investigative techniques that were tried and failed or articulate why such techniques would, most likely, be unsuccessful.

However, even after obtaining a court order authorizing the FBI to install covert listening devices and monitor conversations, steps must be taken to ensure that only conversations about potential violations of criminal law are recorded. If the subject being intercepted hangs up from a call with his business associate wherein they discussed criminal activity and then calls his mother to wish her happy birthday, the call to momma cannot be monitored or recorded. FBI personnel must immediately minimize the intrusion of non-pertinent conversations by terminating the interception, although they may check back in during the call to find out if the topic of the conversation has changed or if new individuals have joined in. To monitor and control how the wiretap is being conducted, the approving judge will require periodic detailed reports regarding the progress and results of the information being obtained and the need to continue the use of electronic interceptions.

Every pertinent call must be recorded and logged into an easily retrieval database. At the conclusion of some long-term investigations, several hundred recordings may have been made. In addition to relying on memory recall, the FBI has developed systems for indexing and accessing specific key words and phrases to ensure investigators and prosecutors are able to put their hands on pertinent testimony. During a trial for a case where hours and hours of conversations were preserved, it is important to know what was said on a recording and what was not captured.

Lawfully authorized electronic surveillance and advanced technology tools are crucial to the FBI's ability to collect evidence and intelligence inside an organization or criminal enterprise too dangerous or operationally impossible to infiltrate.

So, good news! If you are not engaged in felony criminal activity, the FBI won't be wiretapping you. But if you are, you'll be pleased to know that under federal statutes authorizing intercepted communications, you and any third parties overheard will, at some point, be informed that the FBI has been listening to every illicit and conniving thing you've said.

Retired agent J. J. Klaver in episode 123, "Electronic Surveillance, Fort Dix Six Case," talked about being a tech agent on the Technical Operations Squad, collecting evidence and intelligence through the use of lawfully authorized electronic surveillance:

J. J. Klaver (JK): Within the FBI it's referred to as a "TTA," a technically trained agent, and the selection process has evolved over the years. Essentially, once an agent has a minimum of five years of investigative experience [. . .], they can apply through the tech program to become a TTA. Once selected, they then embark on a very intensive training program that is a combination of on-the-job training, what's referred to as "OJT," and specialized classroom training that's conducted down at Quantico and surrounding areas, where parts of the tech program are located. When I went through the training, it was initially a three-week basic electronics class and then an additional five weeks of specialized training. [Those are] the very basics of the tech training and then there's additional specialized training, especially today, as the technologies become much more complicated. Pretty much everything is digital now and Internet based, IT based. Everything is data. So it's a continual learning process as a tech agent. You're continually training, and there is the continuous introduction of new technologies from the FBI.

Jerri Williams (JW): Many of the people listening have no idea what we're talking about. Why don't we give them a little idea of some of the things that a tech agent does?

JK: Every field division has a certain number of tech agents. Big divisions like Philadelphia will have an entire squad of agents. [As a tech agent], you are almost acting in a consulting role. You are applying the FBI technologies in evidence and intelligence collection to pretty much every type of case that the FBI could work. So, you're supporting all of these case agents in the division on all of the squads, be that a drug squad, a public corruption squad, a white collar crime squad, or counter-terrorism. Whatever the squads are that have agents working cases, the tech agents and the tech squad support those agents in the application of the FBI technologies. That includes things such as camera, microphones, audio and data intercepts, tracking devices, and email intercepts. Anything where a case agent needs to collect evidence or intelligence to support their investigation—that's all done through the tech squad when you're talking about the technologies that are used. It's not physical surveillance. That's done by other squads. But it could be electronic surveillance and audio surveillance.

You're either installing microphones or your collecting audio from cell phones or other communication devices, tracking devices concealed and placed on a car or in other packages that are moving and you want to track the location to assist with surveillance. It's a wide variety of collection techniques.

JW: So, when you see in a movie, [people talking] about the FBI having put a bug in the clubhouse of an organized crime group, your team and your squad would have installed that equipment and assisted the case agent with the monitoring devices that would be used to overhear those conversations.

JK: Exactly. The tech agents and the tech squad, they are providing the audio in that instance to the case agent and the case squad. In a situation like that, where you're talking about planting a bug, which could be cameras and microphones to collect both audio and video, a tech squad would gain entry into the location where these were going to be put in. That's referred to as a "surreptitious entry." So essentially, you're breaking into a place, but you're doing it in such a way that the inhabitants of the residence or the people working at the business don't know that you were ever there. It's not like committing a burglary, where you can kick the door in. You have to get in, install your equipment, and get out in such a way that they never know you were there. That means defeating locks and alarms and getting around the dogs or anything that could be an impediment to getting in there unseen. Then you must install the equipment that's going to capture that audio and video. It's going to transmit it out in some form back to a location where it can be monitored under what's called Title 3 of the Federal Criminal Code, which enables law enforcement with a court order to intercept audio and video on a location and then record and monitor it. Now, the tech agents don't monitor or listen to the audio or video; that's up to the case agent and the case squad.

JW: One of the things that you just said that's very important for us to get a little bit more detail on is about getting permission from the court. I think a lot of people have this understanding from books, TV, and movies that show the FBI just tapping people's phones or putting listening devices in their homes or offices. There is so much scrutiny, procedures, and court action that is necessary before we can do that. Can you talk a little bit more about that?

JK: Yes and in fact that is something that is taken very seriously by the entire FBI, but particularly by the tech squad and the tech agents. When you're the agent who is going in and installing a device—and I've done that hundreds and hundreds of times—if there is something illegal about that, then you are the one who could be charged with a federal crime. It is a very serious matter, the unauthorized interception of communications. The tech squad, and the FBI in general, has very strict policies and procedures in place to make sure that all of the legal requirements are met prior to even starting down the path of installing a device that's going to record audio or video or track someone's location. It is something that is taken very seriously. I've never encountered one instance where anything was done without the proper court order, whether that be a search warrant or Title 3 order that allows entry into a place.

———

The method used by tech agents to gain entry into a site can be as simple as pretending to be someone who is supposed to be there, and is hardly noticed.

In episode 087, "Kansas City Mob, Skimming Casinos," retired agent Bill Ouseley explained, with his associate retired detective Gary Jenkins from the Kansas City Intelligence Unit, how tech agents were able to install a bug in a mob boss's meeting place:

Jerri Williams (JW): I want to backtrack a bit because I know everybody is very curious as to how you were able to get those microphones into a club that was frequented by the Kansas City mob. I mean, how does that happen?

Bill Ousley (BO): Well, it's a topic—as you know, Jerri—we don't like to talk about. But in this case, I wouldn't be giving any great technique away because of the way it happened. We called in the experts from Washington, the tech people, when we had something really major. Every office has a tech agent, but when it's a special deal and an entry is going to be possibly difficult, we called headquarters. So they sent out their crew and they had an expert lock picker. They reconnoitered the area; they looked at what kind of lock it was. They do all of their secretive work. Then we put together a plan. In this particular case, the fella from Washington thought he had a particularly easy situation.[. . .] We were looking at the schedule of the opening and closing hours of a restaurant, so we had a pretty good idea when it was going to be closed, and we figured a holiday [would give] us an extra two days. But anyway, that was part of the plan because certainly we can't go in just any night. We needed to know that we were going to have time. So that's scheduled. The tech agent's plan was pretty simple. He and a female agent go over to the location, walking up the street like they may have had a few drinks. They ducked into the doorway of the target restaurant, embraced, and as they were embracing, he picked a lock of the door. That's how they got in.

JW: Wow. And what about everybody connected to the restaurant and the mobsters? How did you know they weren't going to show up all of a sudden?

BO: Well, that's where Gary and his group and our group got together. They assisted us in these installations, and we picked all the logical people who would have to be checked on. While the tech agents did their work, the rest of the squad was on surveillance, watching these people with the help of the Intelligence Unit. In fact, I think you had some people in uniform in case we got in trouble, didn't you, Gary?

Gary Jenkins: Yeah. That was one thing that we always did. When you guys made an entry, usually the sergeant would put on a uniform, check out a marked car, and just kind of sit in the area and monitor your guy's radios and the police radios, just in case somebody called in a suspected burglary.

———

Usually, tech agents make their installations during off-hours. When that's not possible, they'll make sure the real purpose of their presence is never suspected.

Retired agent Marc Ruskin, in episode 081, "False Flag Espionage, Classified Materials Theft," spoke about how tech agents were almost caught installing electronic surveillance equipment in a hotel lobby:

Marc Ruskin (MR): The next day is Tuesday, a Tuesday afternoon. The tech agents are setting up in the lobby of the hotel. They've got a ladder.

They're installing video cameras, and they'd made arrangements with the concierges to have an FBI agent wearing a concierge uniform the next day to greet Oakley [the subject of the investigation] when he comes in with the envelope, with the floppy [disk] so everything can be documented correctly. So there are five tech agents working in the lobby on Tuesday afternoon when who walks in through the door but Oakley, a day early with his envelope and the floppy. The tech agents see him walk in and the one on the ladder almost fell off the ladder when he saw that.

JW: So they were wiring up the lobby preparing for the next day.

MR: Correct. And he shows up a day early. I guess he's so eager to make the deal, he doesn't want to take any chances it's going to go south. So he shows up a day early and the case, right then and there, is almost blown out the window, except for the fact that the tech agents are, of course, dressed in civilian, work-type clothing. He must have just assumed they were making some repairs to the lamps in the ceiling overhead. He walked straight to the front desk, dropped off the envelope, talked to the concierge a little bit, explained, and then walked out. Disaster averted, but just barely. Hindsight tells us that they should have done the installation at three in the morning, not in the middle of the afternoon. But again, that's 20/20 hindsight.

JW: And at this point the concierge is an actual hotel employee and not another agent playing the role.

MR: Correct. So it wasn't as good as it could have been, but at least the concierge was on the ball enough to not ask too many questions.

———

Once the equipment is installed, it's the UCA's responsibility to distract the subjects and persuade them that everything is legitimate and it's safe to talk.

Retired agent Juan Jackson in episodes 072 and 073, "Corrupt Cops, Operation Shattered Shield," discussed the plan he devised to convince the corrupt police officers he was meeting with that they were not being recorded:

Juan Jackson (JJ): It worked out well enough for us to be able to pitch them that I wanted to meet them to discuss how I wanted this operation to go down

Jerri Williams (JW): And where was that meeting?

JJ: This one was in the Hilton Hotel. We had to secure the room, put everything in place that we needed to do to make sure we could record and document this particular meeting. SWAT and everybody else were next door, in case it went bad. All that was set up, securing those two rooms in advance of the meeting.

We did everything we could to put things in place. We had some listening devices in lamps and other things like that. My job was to make sure they sat down where they would face the cameras. You do everything you can by placing chairs and everything there, but you never know what the bad guys are going to do when they come into the room. You're hoping that you can steer them in the right area, so they face the cameras. So they walk through the door and they meet me. I say, "Before we get started, before anybody says or open their mouths, because I don't know you guys and you don't know me, we're all going to strip down to our underwear. That way, I know you don't have on a wire and you're not trying to set me up. You know I don't have a wire on and I'm not trying to set you up." Len was the first one to speak and he said, "Absolutely. Absolutely." He was already leery of the meeting.

JW: Mmmm.

JJ: If we had sat down and started talking without first clearing the air a little bit, then the meeting might not have gone well. So here we go. Of course, all this is recorded. Everybody later got a good kick out of everybody stripping down to their underwear.

JW: You didn't let the case agent or the AUSA know that you were going to do that?

JJ: No.

JW: Did you know that you were going to do it?

JJ: I knew. No one knew but me. And then after that, I told them, because I really felt confident in how well the tech squad worked. I said look around the room, open all drawers and closets. And that's what they did. They started pulling open drawers and lifting up the lamps looking for listening devices or recording devices or cameras planted that they're trying to find. After that, we sat down and Lynn was the first one who opened his mouth. He said, "If you had not done that, I would have not felt comfortable in talking to you."

FBI Film and Fiction Review

White Collar

Neal Caffrey, as played by actor Matt Bomer, is my kind of criminal—a con artist committing scams and schemes all over the world until he's caught by Special Agent Peter Burke, played by Tim DeKay, who has been chasing him for several years. In the 2009-2014 TV series, Caffrey is convicted and sentenced for numerous charges of fraud, forgery, and theft. He is sent to federal prison for four years but escapes from a maximum-security facility near the end of his sentence to look for his missing girlfriend. Agent Burke recaptures Caffrey and offers him a deal: assist the FBI in identifying and apprehending other white-collar criminals instead of returning to prison to serve the remainder of his sentence. For six actioned-packed seasons and eighty-one episodes, the unorthodox duo teams up to solve a wide variety of crimes.

The white-collar crime cases investigated by Agent Burke often made use of electronic surveillance, as is typical in white-collar cases. However, the investigations he and Caffery conducted were a bit more dangerous and violent than the ones I worked on my Economic Crime Squad in Philadelphia. During the series run, the number of con men casualties increased each week. Nevertheless, I enjoyed watching the show before it completed its cable TV run. The show is currently streaming on demand. Perhaps one day I'll binge watch the episodes I missed and relive my glory days chasing fraudsters.

My rating for *White Collar*: I kept my shoes on my feet, but during the show, I loosened the laces just in case.

IT'S COMMON FOR FBI AGENTS TO BE IN GUN BATTLES

Weapons and Shootouts

Shootouts are frequently featured in FBI crime dramas. Although firefights with bad guys do occur, most FBI agents have never fired their weapons in an adversarial situation. This statement is typical of most law enforcement officers. In a Pew Research Center survey conducted by the National Police Research Platform, only a little over a quarter (27 percent) of all officers say they have fired their service weapon while on the job.

FBI agents are required to carry their guns while on duty. According to a historical timeline on the FBI website, agents were granted arrest powers and congressional authorization to carry firearms in 1934, after the murder of an agent during the Kansas City

Massacre of 1933. The timeline notes: "Weapons are necessary tools for a dangerous job—depriving the accused of their liberty and bringing them forward to face justice."

When I joined the FBI in 1982, I was issued a Smith & Wesson .357 Magnum revolver, which I carried in the field for nearly ten years. Most agents are now using a Glock 19, which is a 9 mm semiautomatic pistol as their primary weapon. They also train with and are authorized to carry M16 rifles. Agents must attend at least four mandatory qualification sessions a year under the direction of FBI-trained and -certified firearms instructors. During these training sessions, agents shoot their issued and personally owned weapons and the rifle. They may also shoot the shotgun but only for familiarization; studies have shown that the weapon is not as accurate as the rifle. During my time in the Bureau, the shotgun was the go-to weapon for power and impact. Some of the training sessions include combat courses and shooting at night to replicate all possible situations an agent may encounter in the field. Some firearms instructors also staged "shoot, don't shoot" scenarios at training or at a gun range to give the setting a more authentic feel.

Although well-trained and -equipped, agents accept the incumbent risks of protecting the public. FBI agents have been killed in the line of duty and the FBI honors thirty-six special agents who have died as the result of a direct adversarial confrontation or by the hand of an adversary. As noted in the Wall of Honor tributes on the FBI website, these thirty-six brave agents are memorialized at FBI Headquarters and their respective field offices, so their ultimate sacrifice will always be remembered. I've attended the funerals and visited the gravesites of three of the FBI's thirty-six service martyrs:

- Special Agent Jerry Dove, a classmate and friend from my new agent training class, 82-10 (our class year and class number), was killed on April 11, 1986, in southwest Miami, Florida, during a gun battle with robbery suspects when he and other agents were conducting a mobile surveillance in connection with a series of violent bank and armored-car robberies.

- Special Agent Charles Leo Reed died on March 22, 1996, as a result of gunshot wounds received in Center City Philadelphia in connection with an undercover drug investigation.

- Special Agent Barry Lee Bush was shot and killed on April 5, 2007, in Readington, New Jersey, while working a criminal investigation involving a series of armed bank robberies in central New Jersey.

Attending theirs and countless other funerals for local and state police officers killed in the line of duty has been a stark reminder of the magnitude of the oath of service every law enforcement officer is sworn to uphold.

The most common circumstance for danger is when an agent executes arrest and search warrants. Therefore, planning and preparation are paramount to all FBI tactical operations. Arrests are complex and sometimes volatile operations. It is required that all possible outcomes be considered and anticipated. Case agents must draft a written contingency action plan based on Bureau Standard Operation Policies (SOP) or guidelines for the execution of arrests and searches. This document, which lays out detailed information concerning the subjects and the location, including available medical facilities nearby, is reviewed and approved by field office management prior to the execution. The plan's purpose is to address possible safety and accountability concerns. However, there are factors that can never truly be predicted, primarily and foremost, the independent reactions of the subjects and individuals at the scene.

Retired agent Ed Mireles in episode 118 and 119, "Fatal FBI Miami Shootout," talked about training and muscle memory taking over during a gunfight:

Ed Mireles (EM): So, the lights are flashing. They're giving instructions, and the response was *BOOM, BOOM, BOOM!* That broke the silence. Before I even exited my car, I heard the gunshots. You know, I'm thinking, *God this is incredible.* That's a huge noise. I mean, I knew gunshots. You remember gunshots from firearms training and stuff like that.

Jerri Williams (JW): You know what it's like when you forget to put your ears on at firearms. It's loud.

EM: But you know what? As loud as that was, it wasn't loud. I mean, it's kind of weird. Again, that's a survival trait I guess, a fight-or-flight response. No earmuffs. I could hear it, but it wasn't painful. I mean it wasn't so loud that I'm thinking, *Oh my God! I forgot to get my ear muffs.* But again, it's a fight-or-flight response. It's called auditory exclusion. Your hearing dims down a little bit. Some senses go up, some senses go down. I've been around gunshots without ear protection, and you practically jump out of your skin: "Whoa, what the heck was that!" This time I knew what is was and I wasn't jumping and it didn't hurt. I felt no pain. That's why I didn't know I had been injured. . . My brain was trying to bridge the gap: How did I end up on the ground? I couldn't even conceptualize the idea of getting shot. I'm thinking that I ran into the back of Gordon's car. But it wasn't until I visually examined my arm that I accepted the fact that I had been shot. But I felt no pain. How can you tell you're injured if you feel no pain? Again that's a fight-or-flight response by the human system to getting injured. So, anyway, I just ignored it. Ron said, "Put your gun away. It's over." So, mentally I said okay, and I put my revolver in my holster. And you know, out of all those thousands of hours of training, I snapped the strap on my holster. I snapped that gun in place. All that training, you know muscle memory.

JW: Yeah.

EM: After that, I took about four steps, backed away from the car, and I collapsed and fell on my back.

Shooting Review Teams

All FBI shooting incidents, even the accidental discharge of a weapon by an agent, are investigated and reviewed. When a weapon is fired in a situation involving a criminal matter, a shooting incident review group is deployed to where the shooting occurred, and information is gathered to determine if the agent involved was operating within the scope of the FBI's deadly force policy and in accordance with FBI training and procedures. Agents are permitted to fire their weapons only if they have a reasonable belief that a situation presents an imminent danger of death or serious bodily injury to themselves or others. A simple accidental discharge can be investigated by the special agent in charge. However, if the incident resulted in injuries or fatalities, FBI Headquarters deploys a team to review the incident. All shooting incident reviews are made with the cooperation and assistance of local law enforcement to further determine if any local or state laws were violated.

As is the case in any other type of investigation, all employees, personnel, and witnesses at the scene are identified and interviewed regarding the incident. Investigators also look for safety and training issues that may be revealed during their inquiry. The completed report is reviewed independently by the Shooting Incident Review Group (SIRG), within the Bureau's Inspection Division, to analyze and evaluate the application of deadly force in such incidents.

In episode 161, "Broad Street Shootout," retired agents Jim Sweeney and Richard Macko talked about the Philadelphia homicide and FBI's investigative review of the deadly shootout that left two bad guys dead and seriously injured two agents:

Jerri Williams: Before we move on to the trial, could you talk a little bit about the shooting review? I think that's one thing the public doesn't understand: how seriously the Bureau takes any discharge of a weapon and what's done to conduct an internal investigation.

Jim Sweeney: Well first of all, because there was a homicide, nobody in Philadelphia was allowed to be involved in the shooting review. It's done by FBI inspectors who are just normal supervisors who are trained to do inspections. They get picked to do shooting-team duty, and they were all sent here to Philadelphia. So in theory, nobody knew anybody here, and they're outside objective people coming in to do the shooting review. A lot of us had been through it before in 1990, when we had the Red Roof shootout. But in addition to the Bureau doing their review, because it was classified a homicide, the district attorney's office has to do a homicide investigation. Eventually, the office got a letter from the district attorney saying that the homicide committed by the agents was justified. That was done within a month. The FBI shooting review didn't clear us until August. So, we had the shooting in March, the DA's office rules justified in April, and then finally the Bureau came through in August and also said justified.

Richard Macko: We had to give sworn, signed statements. Mine was taken while I was still in the hospital, on the Friday before I left. The Bureau people came right up to do that.

SWAT and HRT

Being a member of an FBI Special Weapons and Tactics (SWAT) team is a collateral duty. A SWAT team member's primary job is to work investigations. They are street agents first and are assigned to a squad where they investigate specific violations under the Bureau's jurisdiction. SWAT duties are second to their regular responsibilities. Office management is supportive of agents on SWAT and allows them flexibility to be dispatched to critical incidents. Time away from working their cases is also authorized for training. SWAT team members train together several times a year to maintain skills and be prepared to respond wherever and whenever the SWAT team is called out on a mission.

The Bureau has designated a number of SWAT teams in major metropolitan areas, such as New York, Los Angeles, Washington, DC, and Miami, as enhanced SWAT teams. The SWAT teams in these offices make themselves available for missions anywhere in the world. They, therefore, receive additional funding, resources, and training to be able to travel overseas at a moment's notice. SWAT team members are referred to as "operators." Each team has members who specialize in specific techniques and entry methods. Every team has at least one medic.

A SWAT team assigned to a field division is different than being a member of the FBI's Hostage Rescue Team (HRT), a tactical unit capable of responding to major critical incidents throughout the United States and the world. HRT is a tier-one counterterrorism team. Members are full-time, with no investigative duties. Their priority is to train daily at the FBI

Academy in Quantico, where they are based, or at training venues around the world. They train with elite teams in the U. S. military and with some of their foreign counterparts, engaging in the best training opportunities available, such as explosive breaching, fast roping, and survival and para rescue, to ready themselves for whatever terrorist attack or critical incident might happen next, or to bring stability to areas devastated by natural disasters. The HRT also provides protection to dignitaries and security at major events like the Olympics and the Super Bowl.

"The missions are going to remain the same. There's a greater emphasis, of course, on the threat from terrorism. There's a greater emphasis in international deployments. But at the same time, the HRT has deployed to quite a few domestic situations over the past twenty years. So the missions are not going to change that much. The equipment has gotten better— that's to their advantage. Some of the weaponry has changed... The shoulder weapons have changed... As far as the warrior mentally, the physical requirements, and all the other characteristics that I've discussed, those have not changed. Those are the same."

> **—Retired agent Jim McGee, episode 051,**
> **"HRT, FCI Talladega Hostage Rescue"**

The HRT and field SWAT teams carry the same automatic pistols, Glock 9 mm, as do FBI street agents. HRT and SWAT operators also carry sniper rifles.

Retired agent Bill Vanderpool, episode 145, "Guns of the FBI, Firearms Training," discussed the firearms mistakes he sees in TV shows, books and movies:

Jerri Williams (JW): Because of your expertise in FBI weapons and firearms training, when you watch a TV show or a movie, or read a book about the FBI, and there's a scene about guns and shootouts, what are your thoughts? What makes you roll your eyes because it's so inaccurate?

Bill Vanderpool (BV): Well, as far as firearms are concerned, a lot of the actors really don't look like they are shooting. They don't look at their sites at long ranges as carefully as they should. But one of my absolute pet peeves on any cop show is when they'll have a semiautomatic handgun, and they'll enter a building with it. They'll go down two or three hallways and then they get in front of a door they think this guy's behind. That's when they rack a round in the chamber. That's, of course, crazy because you're not going to go into a dangerous situation without the gun fully loaded. Strangely enough, even with my loss of hearing from shooting for so many years, when I watch a television program or a movie where they rack a round into a shotgun, I can hear the fact that they did not actually chamber a round. It didn't have that extra click. So you get used to those things. And then the guns they use are not correct in a lot of cases. My

183

daughter says she can always tell a book that [I've read because there are] little cross outs and little marginal notes with all the mistakes. I've been asked by a lot of different authors to read their books ahead of time to check it for accuracy, and I do that gladly.

JW: What are some of the biggest mistakes that you see in books that you've read?

BV: Basically the handling of the gun or the fact that the gun is misnamed. For instance, the guns we use today are in millimeters. And the basic one is a 9 millimeter. That is not a percentage point. You don't have a decimal point in front of the nine. It's just the regular number 9 millimeter. But you see people with a .9 millimeter. Well, technically speaking, that bullet would be about the diameter of a very thin needle. Little things like that. They could have asked someone to look it over and found some of the mistakes ahead of time.

FBI Film and Fiction Review

Shooter

Actor Mark Wahlberg plays military veteran Bob Lee Swagger in this 2007 conspiracy action thriller. When Swagger is set up as the sniper who, during an assassination attempt against the President of the United States, inadvertently shot and killed the

Ethiopian archbishop, the only one who eventually believes he is innocent is rookie FBI Special Agent Nick Memphis (played by actor Michael Peña). The two men join forces to determine who framed Swagger and why. Swagger, a marksmen and trained mercenary, sets into motion a revenge plan that results in an implausibly high body count.

This big-budget movie was filmed in Philadelphia, and I had the opportunity to work with the production crew, actor Michael Peña, and director Antoine Fuqua during the filming of the assassination scene, which took place on the mall in front of Independence Hall. Members of the Violent Crimes squad were technical advisers for the scenes depicting an FBI SWAT team. I must confess that a large group of Philadelphia Division support employees and my middle-school-age twin daughters were extras in the movie. Admitting that my opinion may be compromised by my personal association with the movie, I didn't think the movie was that bad.

My rating for *Shooter*: I loosened the laces on both shoes, and at the end, I managed to still have one on.

#15

FBI AGENTS FLY AROUND THE WORLD CONDUCTING INVESTIGATIONS

Domestic Investigations

TV shows often have scenes where agents are hopping onto to private planes to be shuttled to meeting and interviews in the United States and around the world. One of the most significant domestic advantages of the FBI is its multistate jurisdiction and ability to pursue investigations across state lines. However, this doesn't mean that agents assigned to cases with witnesses and documents around the country can simply jump on a plane to conduct interviews and gather evidence. Due to case efficiencies and budget constraints, many investigations require that requests for investigation be sent to FBI offices throughout the country. Such a request is known as a "lead" and are assigned by the other office to a lead agent who interviews witnesses, conducts surveillances, or obtains documents on behalf of agents assigned to the originating office (OO).

For example, if an agent in Philadelphia needs a car rental representative in Chicago interviewed about a vehicle used in a bank robbery, but she can't convince her supervisor or ASAC to spend the money to send her, she'll instead prepare a communication to have an agent in Chicago conduct the interview for her. If necessary, she'll call the other agent to give him a clear idea of what details and documents she seeks. When travel is appropriate and authorized, she is required to notify that field office of her presence in the territory. The FBI's fifty-six field offices are headed by a special agent in charge (SAC) or assistant director in charge (ADIC) who would not be happy if an FBI agent from another division was conducting investigations without making notification. And you can rest assured the agent is not flying around on a private jet. That agent flying out to Chicago has a roundtrip ticket on a commercial flight with an economy seat.

There are exceptions. The FBI does own and lease planes for immediate deployment to respond to crisis events all over the world. If necessary, agents on rapid deployment or fly teams may hop a ride on a military transport or even on the FBI director's G5.

International Investigations

As in the case with domestic travel, most investigations in foreign countries are conducted by an agent sending a lead to one of the FBI's approximately sixty overseas offices, called legal attachés (LEGATs). These agents are the personal representatives of the director of the FBI abroad. LEGATs also have approximately two dozen suboffices in key cities around the globe providing coverage for more than 180 countries, territories, and islands. Each office is established through mutual agreement with the host country and is situated in the U.S. embassy or consulate in that nation. The majority of these offices are staffed with only a small contingency of agents, two or three, and one or two support personnel. In addition to covering leads, the purpose of having the FBI represented in these outposts around the world is to uphold the core mission to protect Americans back home by developing and fostering strong liaisons with foreign law enforcement, intelligence, and security services all over the world.

From the FBI Website

"Contact Us"
Overseas Offices

Our legal attaché program is managed by the International Operations Division at FBI Headquarters in Washington, D.C. This office keeps in close contact with other federal agencies, Interpol, foreign police and security officers in Washington, and national and international law enforcement associations. International liaison and information sharing are conducted in accordance with executive orders, laws, treaties, Attorney General Guidelines, FBI policies, and interagency agreements.

(https://www.fbi.gov/contact-us/legal-attache-offices)

As you can imagine, this system can be slow and frustrating. In the movies agents can go anywhere they want and interview anyone they want in a foreign country. But that's the movies, not real life. Depending on the workload, the location of the LEGAT, and the Bureau's relationship with the particular foreign country, the turnaround time for obtaining the results of an investigative request may be lengthy.

"When you deal with LEGATS, legal attachés, it's a pain. Because what I would have to do is send a lead

to London and then they'd have to get it and then they'd go to the Swedish police and ask them to interview the witness in Sweden. So whenever you send a lead internationally, unless it's terrorism or something, it takes six months at least to get an answer back."

—Retired agent Mike Carbonell, episode 015, "Toddler Kidnapped for Ransom and Ira Einhorn"

If an FBI agent needs to travel to a foreign country to interview a witness or subject, she must first submit an official request through the Department of Justice to obtain host country clearance. In many situations, upon approval and arrival in the foreign country, the agent is still not authorized to actually conduct the investigation but optimistically anticipates that they will be allowed to accompany the foreign country's law enforcement officials during the interviews and investigation. If this request is denied, the FBI's foreign-based legal attachés will instead arrange for an official list of questions to be provided to foreign police or security officials who will conduct the interview and report back to the FBI.

I experienced this myself while conducting an international advance fee investigation. The Iranian financier I needed to interview was living in France. However, France is one of those nations that frown on the FBI coming into their country and conducting investigations. So, we instead asked our witness to travel to Spain, where the LEGAT was able to assist our team, the AUSA assigned to prosecute the case, my Postal Inspector partner, and a court stenographer. The LEGAT made the arrangements for us to hold our deposition at his office in the U.S. Embassy in Madrid. He even arranged for telephonic connection with our target and the defense attorney back in Philadelphia.

———

At times, it also possible to take investigative steps while continents away from the action.

In episode 007, "Tracking Top Ten Fugitives," retired agent Jeff Covington explained what an Unlawful Flight to Avoid Prosecution (UFAP) warrant is while talking about working on a Violent Crimes Task Force:

Jeff Covington: Whether someone is a fugitive is determined by local enforcement. This person has committed a violent crime somewhere and then has fled the jurisdiction. The FBI gets involved in these things when a UFAP warrant is issued under Title 18 United States Code Section 1023. What it allows the FBI to do, is to work with local partners and take that felony warrant for a guy wanted for murder once we have some indication that person has fled. As soon as he crosses that state line, he is considered an unlawful flight candidate. We take the local warrant, go to the magistrate and, with the approval of United States attorney's office, a federal UFAP warrant is issued and is good forever and wherever the fugitive goes in the States or the world, we can pursue him or her.

One quick story: We had a guy that committed a homicide. He left the state, so we had an unlawful flight warrant issued for him. That was the job of the FBI agents on the task force, to obtain the UFAP warrants. We thought the guy had fled to Australia. How were we going to get him down there? Well, FBI agents are in fifty-six cities in the United States, but also have a presence in more than sixty countries around the world in the FBI's legal attaches offices. These overseas FBI offices don't have law enforcement powers, but they do have something very powerful, liaison with foreign law enforcement and security agencies. The FBI must depend on the cooperation of foreign agencies such as the New Scotland Yard or even the KGB.

The guy was hiding out in Canberra, Australia, and he called his mom on Mother's Day. We were on his mom's phone. We got the phone number he was calling from in Canberra. In furtherance of that UFAP warrant, that was something we could do under that statute. We sent a communication to the LEGAT in Australia, and he contacts the royal constabulary in Canberra, Australia. They kicked the door in, and our boy was there. They arrested and took him into custody on the strength of that unlawful flight warrant issued in Philadelphia. We contacted the Philadelphia Police Department, and they took an eight-thousand-mile trip to pick him up. The FBI didn't go. That's part of the agreement—that the locals who issued the original warrant had to transport the fugitive back to the States to stand trial for murder in Philadelphia.

It was all accomplished under the power of the FBI and its relationships and associations with these allied organizations. Philadelphia (Police) would not have been able to conduct that fugitive investigation overseas.

Extraterritorial Jurisdiction

Extraterritorial jurisdiction establishes an exception to the policies and procedures of investigating a case overseas.

In the mid-1980s, Congress passed laws that authorized the FBI to investigate when Americans are attacked overseas during a terrorist attack. If there is a bombing, a hostage taking, or a kidnapping of an American and the incident is related to terrorism, the FBI has been granted, through congressional legislation, what is called "extraterritorial jurisdiction." At the invitation of and concurrence and cooperation of the country where the incident occurred, FBI investigators may enter the country and actually conduct investigations. Although extraterritorial jurisdiction provides the authority of the United States to criminalize actions that occur outside of the American borders and then investigate and prosecute them, the statute does not and cannot authorize the encroachment of the sovereignty of the country where the activity occurred. It must be stressed that to work these overseas investigations and partner with that nation's law enforcement and security personnel, the FBI must first obtain permission from the host government to enter the country.

From the FBI Website

"What Happens When An American is Harmed Overseas"

When Americans are seriously harmed overseas, the appropriate US government agencies quickly pull together a coordinated response to the incident. And the FBI often plays a critical role in that response, whether there's one victim or hundreds. We get permission from the host government and always work with that nation's law enforcement and security personnel, in concert with the US Embassy and the ambassador. Our jurisdiction doesn't extend to nonterrorism-related homicides, robberies, rapes, and muggings of Americans—these are usually handled by local authorities. But we can—and sometimes do—offer investigative or forensics assistance in these cases if asked.

(https://archives.fbi.gov/archives/news/stories/2008/june/international_060308)

The FBI may also enter into an extraterritorial investigation at the direct invitation of a foreign nation seeking access to the Bureau's expertise and substantial investigative resources and personnel. In response to these requests for assistance, the FBI may send a fully equipped fly team of first responders to the crime scene or disaster site. FBI critical incident managers trained to handle crisis logistics are ready at a moment's notice to rapidly deploy boots on the ground anywhere in the world. In addition to investigators, these human resources include analysts, hostage negotiators, evidence response teams (ERT), and fingerprint examiners, as well as SWAT or HRT tactical teams for safety and security of the FBI personnel working in the country.

Working successfully overseas is primarily about the relationships established between the FBI and its law enforcement and security partners. Maintaining and nurturing those liaisons is the key.

Retired agent Lauren Anderson in episode 156, "Casablanca Bombings, Paris LEGAT," explains how the FBI coordinates its overseas activities with the State Department and CIA:

Jerri Williams: There may be people listening who don't know the responsibilities of the State Department and how the FBI must coordinate its overseas investigations through the State Department and the embassies. So could you just quickly explain, so they understand?

Lauren Anderson: Yes, that's a great point. Thanks for having me clarify that. So, when an FBI agent is assigned to an embassy or consulate overseas, although they are subordinate to the director, they are considered the director's personal representative, much like an ambassador is the president's personal representative. We are, however, subordinate to the chief of mission, also known as the ambassador, which means we have to keep that individual briefed. Now, the State Department's regional security officer (RSO)—who has the same 1811 job category as FBI agents—is responsible for the security of the embassy itself, the classified documents, and the embassy staff. In most embassies, they are supported by a marine security guard contingent. We had one in Morocco. The RSO's role was to account for all the Americans and account for the security of the facilities and ensure that every single person, if they were at home or somewhere else, were safe and if they needed protection, they got protection. That's largely their role. They can get involved in investigations, but their role is typically to ensure the security of the embassy, the embassy personnel, and classified material.

The chief of station for the CIA is the primary person responsible and the primary point for relationships with the intelligence services in any given country.

They are the lead, just like the FBI is the lead in the United States. So, if we're doing our jobs effectively, we coordinate extremely well with them. Where there is a difference and where there is a line in the sand—and it's true in every country and it's how each of us had to negotiate that—is when something is considered criminal activity. Going back to 1985 and 1986, there was legislation passed that gave the FBI extraterritorial jurisdiction to investigate, respecting the sovereignty of other countries, a certain category of crimes, acts of terrorism, kidnapping, hostage taking, and homicides in the conduct of those activities. On paper, without knowing if we had American victims, clearly this would have been an FBI lead, if the Moroccans allowed us to work with them. That's key. The CIA can be there. But in the countries that I have worked in, the countries would keep talking to the CIA until you cross that line where you're going to start dealing with prosecutors in the judicial system. Then, often times, the CIA has to take a step aside and the primary information comes to the FBI. So, for example, in France, once that line was crossed with a terrorism case, they knew they weren't going to talk to the CIA anymore. I mean they are as a practical matter, but all the information is going to go through the FBI and funneled to the CIA station, so it's a little bit complex.

———

The FBI realizes that by sharing investigative knowledge and providing training for their foreign counterparts, the evidence collection methods used overseas will meet similar standards used by law enforcement in the United States.

Retired agent Bob Clifford in episodes 096 and 097, "Hijacking, Egypt Air Flight 648," explained how the FBI offers to assist foreign government with overseas investigation, allowing agents to preserve evidence:

Bob Clifford: Again, this is late 1985. Earlier that year, for the first time in US jurisprudence, a law was passed giving the United States extraterritorial statutes. Up until that time, Americans could be assassinated, kidnapped, or taken hostage by terrorists overseas and nothing could be done to pursue or prosecute them. And so, Congress passed a law in 1985 that whenever an American is the victim of a terrorist attack, a hostage taking, an assassination, or an attempted homicide, the FBI has the jurisdiction to investigate that crime under the law of the United States. If that foreign location—Bolivia, Malta, Greece, wherever this attack has occurred—if a prosecution is not possible— either because the country lacks the political will or the judicial infrastructure, or just will not prosecute—then this case can be prosecuted in the United States. But we must remember that all the rules of US jurisprudence, all the rules of prosecution, chain of custody, witness testimony, all the items that would take place in a trial in Los Angeles or New York, must be present to potentially try the case in the United States.

But at this time, Malta was going to mount its own prosecution. But because the United States did have some jurisdiction, the FBI offered to assist the Maltese in the investigation, and thankfully that offer of assistance was accepted. So the FBI sent over explosive experts and ballistics experts to lend assistance to the Maltese authorities in that crime scene processing. The reason we do this is because we also want to conduct an investigation in concert with a foreign government, doing our best to protect that prosecution, that evidence, and that testimony, in the event that a prosecution for that attack, for whatever reason, could be mounted in the United States.

———

Working together on matters of common interest allows each country to combine their considerable resources to fight terrorism around the world.

Retired agent John Cosenza in episode 016, "Extraterritorial Jurisdiction & Global Threats," talked about working an active terrorism investigation in Italy and other foreign countries:

Jerri Williams (JW): Usually I complain about how TV and movies show the FBI conducting international investigations. They make it seem so easy, when in most cases, it's really just a liaison function. Now I have to eat my words, because in this particular case, it was actually an active investigation. Can you go over that a little bit more and tell us the significance of this case and if there are other cases, especially now after 9/11, where we are working hand in hand with foreign governments and foreign countries on these type of terrorism or counterterrorism cases?

John Cosenza (JC): It happens more today than it did in the past. If we're invited in with a foreign police force or a foreign government, then we can certainly work the case with them. In this particular instance, we were deputized in the specific case. We couldn't receive that type of information on other cases. With the terrorism cases though, a lot of times the Bureau is asked for assistance, and we're ready to provide it. We were always ready to provide it. These cases cross borders. They're international. This case was an example of the early days when there were cells all over Europe. When they would meet, they would all come together with all the heads of the cells. There would be six, seven, sometimes eight police forces involved in the surveillances and the debriefings.

In the bureau today, especially with extraterritorial cases, if there's a crime against an American based on an act of terrorism and it's a friendly country, a lot of times the Bureau will come in and work with them.

We did that in the Khobar Towers bombing in the late 90s. We did it in Dar es Salaam, Tanzania, when the embassy was attacked. We had a whole group of investigators doing interviews and investigations hand in hand with the Tanzanian police forces. It worked out well. They were actually outstanding. They didn't have the equipment or the resources we had, but they were professional policemen and detectives, and we were able to really work well with them.

JW: Can we then assume that as far as France and what's going on in Belgium (referring to terrorist attacks in those countries in March 2016) that there is some type of involvement from the FBI and the United States with those investigations too?

JC: You know what, Jerri? I would assume there's a lot of working together and sharing of information. Other than that, I really don't have the knowledge anymore as to how closely they're working. I would assume that they're sharing quite a bit of information, which is huge.

JW: I hope so.

JC: If you know there are always gaps in investigations and when you can meet with another police force or intel service that can fill those gaps and you can fill gaps for them, that's really important.

———

The restrictions placed on FBI investigators operating in other countries is more easily understood when similar limitations are applied to foreign law enforcement agencies traveling within the United States.

In episode 111, "The Looming Tower, John O'Neill, Yemen, and 9/11," retired agent Ray Holcomb talked about FBI agents being armed while assigned to dangerous overseas posts:

Ray Holcomb (RH): In most of these cases, we were allowed to bring our weapons and carry our weapons, in most of these third world countries.

Jerri Williams (JW): Could you explain why that's significant, that you were allowed to carry your weapon?

RH: Yes, it's very significant because. . .well, reverse this. Imagine, let's say some nationals from another country, some French nationals were attacked and killed in the New Orleans. The French wanted to send an investigative team, and they want their investigators to carry sidearms and maybe even M4 rifles. Can you imagine the reaction of the US government? They would never allow that. Most governments in the world would not allow that. However, a lot of these [terrorist] attacks were taking place in third world countries where they welcomed our assistance, because they were so strapped for resources. These investigations were always spearheaded by the State Department, but they would say to the State Department that they could not guarantee the safety of your FBI people if they come here to work these cases.

The next question then was, would you allow our FBI people to carry their weapons? Oftentimes, we were allowed to. So, here we were in another country packing our weapons. We'd be discreet about it. We made every effort to conceal our weapons, but we were armed. Depending upon where we were going, we would also wear body armor.

FBI Film and Fiction Review

Catch Me If You Can

The 2002 feature crime film *Catch Me If You Can* starred actor Tom Hanks as FBI Special Agent Carl Hanratty, a veteran agent determined to apprehend young con man Frank Abagnale Jr., played by Leonardo DiCaprio. Christopher Walken and Martin Sheen also played roles in the movie, which was directed and produced by Steven Spielberg and DreamWorks. The film was based on the memoir of Frank Abagnale Jr., which recounts his true-life adventures as a check forger when he was a young adult. At the time, he was, allegedly, the youngest person ever to make the FBI's Ten Most Wanted List.

During the movie, young Abagnale skillfully convinces others that he is an airline pilot, a doctor, and an attorney. His successful impersonations allow him to steal millions of dollars while evading capture by Agent Hanratty, who chases him to glamorous locales around the world. The movie portrays Abagnale's exploits and Hanratty's pursuit with action, excitement, and humor. In spite of the fact that Hanratty is played as a typical humorless portrayal of an FBI agent, I enjoyed the film—perhaps because it focused on the scams and schemes I used to investigate.

My rating for *Catch Me If You Can*: No footwear was removed during the viewing of this movie.

#16
FBI AGENTS INVESTIGATE MURDERS

Violent Crime

Most crime dramas about the FBI portray agents heading up the investigation of a local murder. The fact is that in real life, most FBI investigations do not feature a dead body. The lead investigators for most murders are local or state law enforcement officers and the murderers, when apprehended, are tried in state court. There are, of course, circumstances where murder is a violation of federal law and when a murder can be prosecuted in federal court. In these situations, the presence of a corpse is usually not the primary felony the agents are attempting to investigate and solve.

The most common situations where the FBI enters into a murder investigation are when a federal fugitive warrant has been issued for the apprehension of a person known to be responsible for a murder, but who has fled across state lines or out of the country. Based on this information, a local or state police department may request that the FBI file for an Unlawful Flight to Avoid Prosecution (UFAP) warrant to be issued by a federal judge. These warrants allow the Bureau to enter the case and begin a fugitive hunt for the individual at large, using FBI authorized tools and methods to track the target's whereabouts. However, technically speaking, the Bureau's task is the apprehension of the interstate fugitive suspect and the execution of the UFAP warrant, not the investigation of the actual murder. Once arrested, the subject is usually remanded to the custody of the local or state agency and tried in state court.

The FBI authorization to investigate a murder is most clear when the homicide occurs on federal property or on an Indian reservation and under special maritime or territorial jurisdiction, when the murder occurs onboard a US Navy or US Merchant Marine ship in international waters or on US military bases worldwide. These federal laws make murder a federal crime.

But you may be wondering about news reports regarding murder investigations in which the FBI is involved. In these circumstances, there is always a federal violation also in play when the victim was killed, such as a hate crime where the person's civil rights were violated, a teller or security guard is murdered during the robbery of a federally insured bank, or a kidnapping where the victim was taken across state lines. Even with the FBI's participation in an investigation of these types of murder scenarios, as previously stated, it is often determined that the matter be prosecuted in state court, instead of federal court.

There are also a number of violations specifically relating to murder of certain US persons based on their positions and roles in the US government. Under these circumstances, their murders can be charged as a crime under federal laws. These include the murder of the president and other elected or appointed federal officials, such as cabinet members and members of congress. It is also a federal crime to kill a federal judge, a federal prosecutor, or to murder a federal law enforcement official, such as an FBI, DEA, IRS, or Secret Service agent. In order to protect against threats or retaliation intended to influence or coerce the handling or outcome of investigations, these laws also extend to the agent's immediate family members. These cases are rare, but the laws are in place if ever needed.

There are also federal laws enacted to charge murders that occur to promote a criminal enterprise, such as organized crime and drug trafficking as federal crimes. The federal statute Murder in Aid of Racketeering, refers to homicides committed to maintain or increase standing in a criminal organization. In an attempt to protect against the tampering of government processes, specific laws are included to counter intimidation designed to prevent victims, witnesses, sources, and informants from testifying in court. The murders of court officers and jurors in retaliation of testimony given at trial are also federal crimes.

"So the DC police… were kind of at their wits end. They were experiencing so many murders that they were just trying to keep up with the numbers. They asked us to see if we could take him on as a target and that's what we did. He was the first person that was supposed to face the death penalty in DC. Whether or not he would have gotten it would have depended on how good our case would have been, which I think would have been pretty good. Instead, Perry pled guilty to five CCE homicides, which are murders in the furtherance of a Continuing Criminal Enterprise. It's a sort of a drug homicide for lack of anything else you'd call it."

— Retired agent Dan Reilly, episode 077, "Hitman Wayne Silk Perry, Witness Retaliation"

The FBI crime fiction connection to serial killers is supported by federal laws that make murder related to the sexual exploitation and abuse of children and rape or sex crime felony violations. Based on the interstate commerce aspect of the transactions, murder-for-hire, and murder cases where the U S

Postal Service is used to send items to cause the death of the recipient are also federal crimes.

So, yes, the FBI does investigate murder but under specific circumstances. It is important to remember that the FBI does not operate its own local morgue or coroner's office and, therefore, must work closely with local and state first responders, police departments, and medical examiners on all investigations involving a homicide. These are all initially local and state cases that can be worked jointly with the FBI until it is determined if the person responsible will be charged in state or federal court. FBI personnel who participated in the investigation of a murder that is later tried by the state are often invited to be members of the prosecutive team assisting the local district attorney and called as fact witnesses to testify during the trial.

Retired agent Eddie Freyer, in episode 57 and 58, "Polly Klaas, Child Abduction and Murder," discussed working as a member of the prosecution team in a state trial:

Jerri Williams: Could you share with everyone why the state prosecuted this case even though the FBI was so involved in the investigation? Could you talk about the distinctions?

Eddie Freyer: Sure. Quite often the old standard in terms of when the FBI assumes primary jurisdiction on a kidnapping case is whether you have a strong interstate nexus. Usually, that meant your victim was taken across state lines or there was some other very significant interstate aspects to the case, maybe money transferred or some of the subjects in your case were located across state lines. That sort of thing usually gave the FBI a very clear jurisdiction on the case.

This case really did not have any interstate aspects to it. The investigation pretty much confined itself to Northern California. Though we had many counties involved that had witnesses, the suspect, the victim, the crime itself, the body recovery—all the major crime scenes—were confined to Sonoma County or Mendocino County. And so, even though a lot of the work was done by the FBI, a lot of the search warrants were federal search warrants, a lot of the subpoenas, and other court orders were from the federal side of the case. The assumption all along, unless there was some sort of interstate aspect to it, was that we were working on the premise that it would eventually be prosecuted locally.

But that didn't deter the FBI's commitment in this case. Again, reflecting back on the number of cases that were unsolved, I think our commitment was that we needed to solve one. We need to solve one, as grievous as this one, as traumatic as this one. Let's put everything into it and try to solve it, and we were lucky enough to do that.

FBI Film and Fiction Review

Mississippi Burning

Mississippi Burning is an American crime thriller released in 1988. The script is loosely based on the murders of three civil rights activists James Chaney, Andrew Goodman, and Michael Schwerner, who were abducted and murdered in Neshoba County, Mississippi, in June 1964. Actors Willem Dafoe and Gene Hackman play FBI agents Alan Ward and Rupert Anderson, respectively. The two agents are assigned to go to Mississippi to investigate the disappearance of the three civil rights workers. Agent Ward and Agent Anderson attempt to interview potential witnesses, but no one is willing to cooperate, including the local police authorities who don't appreciate the FBI interfering in their business. Fearful of retaliation, even members of the African American community the civil rights workers were there to help are afraid to speak up about what they know. Frustrated with the lack of progress in the investigation, the two agents argue over the right strategy and tactics to motivate people to talk, and at the conclusion of the film, a more aggressive method is successfully used to secure the evidence needed to apprehend those responsible for the deaths.

Despite complaints regarding the movie's deviation from historical accuracy, *Mississippi Burning* was a hit, receiving seven Academy Award nominations, including Best Picture. The film won for Best Cinematography. I agree that the acting was superb. However, the questionable methods used by the agents to obtain confessions provided an inaccurate portrayal of FBI procedures.

My rating for *Mississippi Burning*: I kept my shoes on my feet, but during the movie, I loosened the laces just in case.

#17

A FORENSIC EXAMINER DOES IT ALL— COLLECTS EVIDENCE AND INVESTIGATES

Forensics and Technology

Due to popular investigative TV dramas, some armchair detectives may have unreasonable expectations regarding the collection and analysis of evidence in real-life. They believe that real-life forensics should produce the same results as they do on their favorite show. The most frequently recognized misconception is that DNA and other forensic evidence is always present and can be analyzed quickly. This unrealistic expectation is known in the legal community as the "CSI effect" and has seriously impacted what jurors expect to see presented during trials. Jurors on criminal trials have been known to question why prosecutors did not present the types of forensic evidence that they had seen on TV. They are suspicious of law enforcement officers who did not apply forensic techniques that were created by script writers not scientists. We will address some of these in this chapter.

The *CSI* franchise (see Film and Fiction Review at the end of this chapter), while no longer produced, can still be viewed on cable and streamed on demand. Plus, a brand-new crop of cop shows and investigative dramas exist today to ensure that a new generation is also being "informed" by fictional forensic breakthroughs. In two different episodes of the CBS show *FBI*, the intelligence analyst made references to audio DNA and making a positive identification using biometric software to measure a person's gait, with the statement that the way a person walks is as unique as fingerprints. She was instantly able to positively identify subjects from a voice recording and a grainy surveillance video using facial recognition. That's fun TV stuff, but the application of these emerging technologies for everyday law enforcement use is exaggerated. Creative license was definitely applied in the reliability of these tools. The question is, do most viewers understand this?

The FBI Laboratory

Another thing that TV dramas inaccurately portray is that an FBI field office has its own laboratory facility. There's only one FBI laboratory and it is located in Quantico, VA, on the same site as the FBI Academy. The FBI laboratory provides forensic examinations, technical support, expert witness testimony, training to federal, state, and local law enforcement agencies and operational response to events, such as terrorist attacks and natural disasters, all around the world.

Forensic examiners can be special agents with a science background or, more likely, highly educated scientists and expertly trained technicians. However, a forensic examiner is not a one-stop shop. Unlike on TV, each forensic examiner at the FBI Laboratory has a specialty, whether it be DNA, hair and fibers, fingerprints, ballistics, or blood spatter analysis. They aren't experts in everything. Their testimony is narrow in scope. We discussed composite characters before, where, due to time constraints, one character is developed to represent all the people who would normally be involved. So, in most crime scene dramas, there's usually one forensic examiner who does it all.

The FBI Lab can be used by authorized police departments and provides examinations and testimony in state court at no cost to the summoning law enforcement agencies. FBI personnel from the lab have testified in many high-profile state murder cases in which the FBI's only involvement in the matter was that forensic analysis presented during the trial was conducted at the FBI Lab.

The expectations for DNA analysis is the most challenging misconception. A DNA match can only be made if the suspect's DNA is on file in the Combined DNA Index System (CODIS). The offender index contains DNA profiles of individuals convicted of violent crimes. Unlike the fingerprint identification system, CODIS does not maintain DNA profiles of the general population. The public's interest in DNA analysis has increased with, after many years, the capture of the elusive Golden State Killer based on the use of a public genealogy database to identify him.

Another test of reality is the overall existence of DNA. Sometimes, in real life, no usable DNA evidence can be collected. Sometimes no blood, no hair, no fibers are found at the crime scene, perhaps no fingerprints either. And that's okay. However, investigators and prosecutors must somehow convince jurors and even the victim's family members that no one was negligent. Sometimes no DNA was present or there wasn't enough available to test. Perhaps the suspect was lucky or extra-careful, taking countermeasures, such as wearing gloves or destroying or removing evidence such as rugs and bedding from the crime scene. Bad guys watch *CSI* too.

ERT and Dive Teams

In the field, highly trained FBI personnel assigned to an Evidence Response Team (ERT) collect forensic evidence from crime scenes and searches. In most instances, being on an ERT is a collateral or ancillary assignment, and ERT members are responsible for performing their regular investigative and administrative duties. However, when activated, ERT members use their specialized training to document and collect evidence from crime scenes and crisis situations.

From the FBI Website

"Evidence Response Team"

The ERT program supports teams in all fifty-six FBI field offices. These highly trained and equipped teams operate at an exceptional level of competence to ensure evidence is collected in such a manner that it can be introduced in courts throughout the United States and the world. ERTs strive to be the model for crime-scene processing from the standpoint of safety, expertise, training, equipment, and capability.

(https://www.fbi.gov/services/laboratory/forensic-response/evidence-response-team)

In addition to the ERT, the FBI also assigns and trains employees on Hazardous Evidence Response Teams (HERTs) and Underwater Search and Evidence Response Teams (USERTs), also referred to as "dive teams." These teams provide traditional and hazardous evidence collection capabilities to support FBI investigations.

Handling Evidence and Chain of Custody

Another thing that TV shows and books get wrong or ignore is chain of custody and evidence preservation. It's not enough to pick up an item at a crime scene and drop it into a plastic baggie or tissue pulled from the agent's pants pocket. Requirements are stringent. Evidence must be preserved and sealed in special evidence bags and the handling and custody of the evidence documented. If the chain is broken, it may not be acceptable to be entered as evidence in court.

In real life, an ERT member collecting evidence would carefully photograph and label first, maintaining possession of each item. Handling evidence this way is known as following the chain of custody, where items are maintained from the time they are found at the scene through that time where they may be presented in court as evidence. This ensures that law enforcement has total care and custody of that evidence and that the evidence has not been tampered with and was collected and preserved properly in a secured evidence vault or safe, so the analysis from the evidence can be trusted and relied upon in court.

From the time the evidence is collected in the field, the chain of custody requires it must be strictly handled and maintained, through collection, preservation, and submission. It may first be acquired by a local law enforcement agency before being sent to the FBI Laboratory by the local FBI field office. One single piece of evidence may have several different exams that need to be conducted. As that piece of evidence is transferred throughout the laboratory, chain of custody has to be maintained to make sure that everyone who had control and custody of that evidence is known and documented. Once the evidentiary examinations are complete, the evidence, along with the chain of custody forms is returned to the submitting agencies. The agency will secure the evidence until it is presented at trial. If the chain of custody is broken at any point along the way, the defense may request a suppression hearing and the evidence could be deemed inadmissible in court. Therefore, maintaining the chain of custody is critical to the entire investigation.

Retired agent and former director of the FBI Laboratory Joseph DiZinno, in episode 093, "FBI Laboratory, Katrinak Murder Case," discussed how to safeguard against unreasonable evidence expectations during actual criminal trials:

Jerri Williams (JW): Jurors are expecting things from laboratory analysis that really don't exist. Can you talk to us a little bit about that?

Joseph DiZinno (JD): We're well aware that the jurors watch *CSI*. By watching *CSI* and all the other shows that involve forensic analysis, they come to some degree of understanding a tiny bit of the science. Which means if they're chosen to be a juror on a case, they have an expectation as to how the evidence should be presented because that's how they do it on *CSI*. Generally, that's not the way it is. There is a grain of truth running through those shows about how the exams may be performed, but generally the expectation that the jurors have of the speed and about how the exam is done is nothing like it is in real life. We understand that they expect that and we have to be aware of that when we testified. We explain to them, so they can understand what's being done.

It may be complex science and DNA analysis, but you have to explain it to them so they understand it at a very basic level. So, making sure the jury understands how you do things and a little bit about the science may allay the fears: that your examination wasn't done like *CSI*; therefore, we can't believe it. You need to explain that evidence exams aren't always obtained in six hours and that it takes days, weeks, months sometimes before we have a result in a case. So it's a very real CSI effect. We see it. The bad guys watch *CSI* too and they may take cautions to prevent spreading evidence so it's something that a forensic community is well aware of.

JW: So when you're watching a movie or a TV show or reading a book that talks about laboratory analysis, what are some of the things that really make you want to scream out loud?

JD: Well, one thing is the speed at which things are portrayed on television and sometimes in novels. Many of these techniques take time and a lot of effort in order to perform the examinations. The speed at which they're done in real life as opposed to the speed at which they're portrayed in movies is often far different. That's one thing. The other thing I think is interesting is forensics is a very specialized world. If you're in the FBI laboratory and you're performing nuclear DNA and DNA analysis, that's all you do every day, all day. You don't even perform mitochondrial DNA analysis; it's very specialized. Same if you're doing fingerprint. That's all you're doing is fingerprint examinations. Whereas, on some of these shows on TV, the people who are performing exams do a fingerprint exam, and they might do a hair exam, then they might do a document exam. Then they get in the Learjet, fly across the country, break down the door, and arrest the suspect. That's just not the way it's done. It's very specialized work, not only in the laboratory, but also in the field.

———

In cases where witnesses to a violent crime are too frightened to come forward, forensic evidence may be the only thing to connect a suspect to the victim.

In episode 077, "Hitman Wayne Silk Perry, Witness Retaliation," retired agent Dan Reilly talks about how important forensic evidence can be, especially when investigators can't rely on the cooperation of witnesses:

Dan Reilly (DR): The next thing we found out about was a Mazda van that they were driving around and using. The FBI laboratory referred to it as the "murder van."

Jerri Williams (JW): Great.

DR: Yeah. When we recovered the van, we'd been told that it had been cleaned after the murder of Garrett Terrell, one of the drug dealers that worked for Martinez. We had our forensics team go over it from top to bottom. They said it looked like more than one person had been murdered inside the van. We did recover a bunch of blood off the back of the front driver's seat. I thought, based on the information that we started to develop about how the murder happened, that blood should have been Garrett Terrell's blood. But unfortunately, we ended up with a lab report that said, found on Terrell's body were unique carpet fibers from the van, not only carpet fibers from the storage area of the van, which was the back sort of baggage compartment of the van, but also carpet fibers from the front part of the van. So, in other words, two unique styles of carpet fibers that were on Terrell's body.

JW: So you knew definitely that he had been in that van.

DR: Yes. We knew he had been in the van. We also found in the van fibers from the clothing he had worn that night. We also found his fingerprints in the van. So, we knew he was in the van. That was how we were starting to put the things together in terms of forensics. It was frustrating for me at the time because DNA was brand new in terms of usage in our cases. At that point, I was frustrated by the fact that we didn't have Terrell's DNA inside the van. I knew anything we came up with, we were going to have to have significant forensic evidence to prove a case against Perry. We were in a position where we weren't going to be able to rely very much on civilian witnesses, regular witnesses.

Kearney (a cooperating witness) said he thought the only place that Terrell's blood could have ended up would be down in the passenger side rear wheel area. So I went back into the van, after all those months that we'd had it, and went back into the wheel well area. Sure enough, there was a whole pool of blood down at the bottom of the wheel well. I recovered several blood samples from that pool of blood and resubmitted those for the DNA and, of course, it matched Terrell. That's really what closed the gap on the forensics that we had.

———

Agents who have received extensive training on the proper procedures used to collect evidence, are especially frustrated by scenes in movies and on television not adhering to protocol.

Retired agent Debra LaPrevotte in episode 151, "Kleptocracy, International Corruption, and Recovering Human Remains," talks about *CSI* and the evidence collection mistakes she sees on TV show:

Jerri Williams (JW): Is there anything that you see, say in a TV show or in a movie, that has to do with evidence collection that just makes you roll your eyes and say, "That's not how it works?"

Debra LaPrevotte (DL): I'm a big fan of *CSI*. The original, not the five copycat shows, but the original. But yes, it's when they would be walking through a house with a flashlight, when they could simply turn the light on. I get it. It's much more dramatic walking to a crime scene with a flashlight. But seriously, it's night; the crime's already happened. Obviously, if they're there, they have a search warrant or some probable cause to be on the property. They're not looking for the suspect and they're still walking through with a flashlight. They could just flick the switch and turn the light on, right? Because, as all the ERT people out there know, you photo in and you photo out. They should be taking photographs, and they can't do that with the lights off. It's that or when people go into a crime scene by themselves.

JW: Oh yeah.

DL: I was at the Academy watching *The Silence of the Lambs* and laughing with the rest of the class, thinking, sure, let's not get somebody with twenty years of experience. Let's pull somebody out of new agent class and have them investigate a complex serial murderer. Of course, she goes into a storage facility by herself. It's that kind of thing. Or they're not wearing gloves. Our photographers are wearing gloves because somebody is going to have to touch something. It's little things like that, that irk me when I'm watching some of the crime shows.

And another thing; just because you see a dead body doesn't mean you have probable cause to enter the house. I mean, you still need a warrant. The guy's dead. No exigent circumstances exist. Explaining to them about plain view doctrine, if you can see something in plain view, then yeah you can search there.

FBI Film and Fiction Review

CSI: Crime Scene Investigation

CSI was a TV franchise that aired on CBS for fifteen years from 2000-2015. The series did not feature the FBI or FBI agents, but is included in *FBI Myths and Misconceptions: A Manual for Armchair Detectives* due to the significant impact it had on real-life forensics and how the evidence collected for FBI cases is often scrutinized as a result of the unreasonable expectations of jurors who have watched the TV show.

During its time, the original show, *CSI: Crime Scene Investigation*, also known as *CSI: Las Vegas* (starring well-known actors William Petersen, Marg Helgenberger, and Ted Danson) spun off into a franchise located in two additional American cities, *CSI: Miami* (2002-2012) and *CSI: NY* (2004-2013). The first three CSI series followed the work of forensic scientists who determined the causes and culprits involved in the strange deaths featured on each episode. Cyber forensics and behavioral psychology were showcased in the fourth spin-off, *CSI: Cyber* (2015-2016). Each forensic team member did it all; collected and analyzed the evidence from a wide variety of crime scenes and conducted the investigations that solved the crimes. These four shows were popular with television viewers, but presented fictional laboratory techniques and nonexistent forensic methods and cyber procedures that, unfortunately, viewers believe are factual.

My rating for *CSI*: Has anyone seen my shoe?

———

Bones

On each episode of the FOX Television crime drama *Bones*, the subject matter, dead bodies and human remains, was always morbid and often unpleasant. However, the show was also a love story, albeit one with many dark comedic moments. The drama was produced by crime novelist Kathy Reichs, who, in addition to writing books, is a forensic anthropologist and former professor. The main FBI character was Special Agent Seeley Booth, played by David Boreanaz. Fortunately for him, the FBI had on retainer the services of forensic anthropologist

Dr. Temperance "Bones" Brennan, played by actress Emily Deschanel.

During the series' twelve seasons (2005-2017), the world-renown FBI Laboratory was delegated to a back-seat role as Dr. Brennan and her colorful team of scientists at the fictional Jeffersonian Institute worked alongside Agent Booth to provide complex and innovative scientific analysis to help him solve cases. Although in real life, a gun-toting forensic anthropologist would never be partnered with an agent in the field, and the FBI Lab would have handled most of the scientific investigative analysis featured on *Bones*, the Bureau, at times, has collaborated with and utilized the expertise of scientists at the Smithsonian Institution. In episode 160 of *FBI Retired Case File Review*, retired agent Warren Flagg spoke about investigating a pet cemetery scam where, during the trial, the Smithsonian Institution provided a deposition determining the identification of dog and cat bones from an illegal mass cremation.

My rating for *Bones*: I kept my shoes on my feet, but during the show, I loosened the laces just in case.

#18 BOMB TECH IS A DANGEROUS JOB

Special Agent Bomb Techs (SABT)

Of course, anyone handling sensitive blasting caps, potentially unstable chemicals, and homemade explosives is encountering potential risks. However, the image often shown on TV of a MacGyver-type character cutting green and red wires while attempting to dismantle a bomb is an inaccurate cliché. Technology, such as remote equipment, has significantly increased the safety margin for a bomb technician, a specialized law enforcement position. There are two primary responsibilities for an FBI Special Agent Bomb Technician, known as a SABT:

1. They coordinate liaison, training, and response with their local police and military counterparts.

2. They routinely respond with their law enforcement partners to calls about suspicious packages and bomb threats.

They conduct these duties whether or not there is a federal nexus or connection. SABTs are always standing by supporting the local police departments on-site at major events such as the Super Bowl, the Olympics, political conventions, holiday parades, and even the Academy and Emmy Awards. Based on their assessments of the post-blast crime scenes they process, SABTs may also be called to testify in court.

All but the smaller FBI offices have one or more full-time SABT.

"Essentially you've got what's called left of boom and right of boom. Left of boom is everything you've done before the suspicious package or IED functions as designed. Then you've got right of boom. That means the device has functioned before the bomb squad has gotten there and now we have a crime scene."

—Retired agent Kevin Miles, episode 086, "Master Bomb Technician, Khobar Towers Attack"

Suspicious Packages and Bomb Threats

At one time, a bomb tech wearing a bomb suit and carrying X-ray equipment would approach a suspicious package to determine what it was. Nowadays, however, it is rare for a bomb tech to directly handle a suspicious package or an unexploded improvised explosive device (IED). Safety is at the forefront. Remote equipment is used to examine possible explosive devices and, if needed, to render them safe. Everyone is evacuated to a safe zone and a robot is engaged to carry the suspicious package to where a powerful water charge can remotely disable or detonate the device.

Post-Blast Crime Scenes

When the SABTs arrive after a bomb has exploded, they spend their time monitoring the post-blast crime scenes. The actual site is processed by the Evidence Response Team, all of whom are also post-blast trained. However, the SABTs are present as specialists trained to examine items recovered from the crime scene and quickly determine, say from how a piece of metal was bent and shaped, if it is significant evidence in relation to the bombing. If the matter goes to trial, a SABT will be asked to testify as an expert witness, explaining in state or federal court what the explosive device was made of, how it was constructed, how it functioned, how close it was to the detonation, and other pertinent identifiers. It should be noted that explosives examiners back at the FBI Laboratory in Quantico who receive evidence from the field are responsible for testing the items for explosive residue materials and for providing expert testimony about the chemical elements of a bomb. In most cases, they are able to analyze and determine the composition of the explosive device.

FBI bomb techs also provide training to the military and law enforcement partners in such specific disciplines as Basic and Tactical Post-Blast School, Large Vehicle Bomb Post-Blast School, and Underwater Post-Blast Crime Scene School. One of the most important lessons taught is how to avoid contaminating the crime scene by always wearing gloves, Tyvek suits, and protective shoe covering.

Weapons of Mass Destruction and InfraGard Coordinators

In addition to SABTs, the FBI has weapons of mass destruction and InfraGard coordinators dedicated to monitoring the use of destructive devices that could cause harm and mayhem on a large scale. InfraGard is a partnership between the FBI and the private sector, and members share information to mitigate threats to our nation's critical infrastructures and key resources.

From the FBI Website

"What We Investigate—Weapons of Mass Destruction"

Each FBI field office has a weapons of mass destruction (WMD) coordinator whose primary function is to coordinate the assessment of and response to incidents involving the use or threatened use of chemical, biological, and radiological/nuclear materials. Each WMD coordinator is tasked with establishing appropriate liaison with regional, state, and local emergency response personnel as well as with critical facilities within each field office's jurisdiction in order to facilitate notification and response to WMD incidents.

(https://www.fbi.gov/investigate/wmd)

Most FBI divisions also sponsor within their territory one or more chapters of InfraGard. According to the InfraGard website, there are currently eighty-two chapters throughout the United States. Members representing private companies, universities, military and government agencies, cyber professionals, and state and local law enforcement meet to discuss threats and other matters that impact their organizations, provide industry-specific insights, and advance national security.

Retired agent Kevin Miles, episode 086, "Master Bomb Technician, Khobar Towers Attack," discussed the movie *Hurt Locker* and working as an FBI master bomb tech:

Jerri Williams (JW): I learned everything I know about being a bomb tech from watching the movie, Hurt Locker.

Kevin Miles (KM): Ugh! Ha-ha. Okay.

JW: Did you see it?

KM: I actually watched that movie in a small theater in Beverly Hills, California, when it first—actually before it came out.

JW: Oh, excuse us.

KM: Yeah. I was invited by *60 Minutes* to come and view it with a whole bunch of other military bomb technicians...to get our take on it. Actually, the director was there, and the writer was there as well. We watched it, and I'll reserve judgment on that.

JW: I really liked the movie, but I guess this is going to be great because you're going to be able to tell us some of the things that are misconceptions. So, let's get into that. Why would anybody in the world want to become a bomb tech? It sounds like a very dangerous occupation to me.

KM: It's not as dangerous as people think. Back in the olden days, before robots, before bomb suits, yeah, it was pretty dangerous. You didn't have the equipment that you have nowadays. All that people know about bomb squads and bomb technicians is what they see in the movies, e.g., *The Hurt Locker*, where people are doing things that in real life are very rarely, if ever, done anymore. In a lot of ways, being a police officer or a firefighter is even more dangerous than being a bomb technician because we know what we're doing, and we know what we're facing. We have the equipment, we have the training, and we know what we're getting into. So, I mean it's a dangerous job, but it's not as dangerous as it used to be.

When I first came on the bomb squad, we didn't have robots and we didn't have anywhere near the equipment we have now. And there was a lot of what's called "hand entry" which means actually putting your hands on suspected IEDs or real IEDs and taking them apart by hand. That's not done anymore. And if it is, it's a very, very, very rare occurrence.

So anyway, it was very fascinating. I've always told people that being an FBI bomb tech, being a SABT is, without doubt, the best job in the Bureau. And the reason is no one knows what you do and they're afraid to ask. A lot of time, they give you a lot of latitude. They say, "Please don't blow yourself up, and please don't blow up our vehicles." If you know what you're doing, abide by your training, and use your equipment the way it's supposed to be used, you'll be fine.

———

In the United States, explosives can be purchased by companies with proper ID, licenses, and storage facilities. According to Master SABT Kevin Miles, there are only two other ways to acquire explosives; steal them or make them. During my career, I did not have the opportunity to be present at a post-blast crime scene, but I enjoyed hearing the stories recounted by the Philadelphia SABT and his bomb-sniffing dogs.

FBI Film and Fiction Review

The Kingdom

The Kingdom is a 2007 star-studded movie about a team of elite FBI agents sent to Saudi Arabia to solve a mass bombing and find the terrorists responsible before they strike again. The movie starred Jamie Foxx and Jennifer Garner as ERT trained agents. Chris Cooper played the bomb technician.

The film did a great job of showing how an FBI team deployed overseas conducts a post-blast crime scene investigation. I was told that the production team and Chris Cooper spent time with FBI bomb techs and the ERT members assigned to the Los Angeles Division preparing for those roles before filming began. It was obvious to me that they put a lot of effort into making the movie appear as real as possible. I recognized several scenes apparently inspired by the real-life investigations of the Khobar Towers and USS Cole bombings.

As portrayed in *The Kingdom*, FBI ERT members can be deployed around the world at only a moment's notice, however, not without State Department approval and host country clearance. In the movie, a US senator attempts to stop FBI ERT deployment when in reality it would have been the ambassador who had the authority to deny FBI entry into Saudi Arabia. The film was accurate in showing that, in most instances, the agents are not allowed to carry their weapons overseas. However, they would not have handed them over to a foreign law enforcement agency. To evaluate the accuracy of the post-blast crime scene actions of the agents with boots on the ground, I called retired agent Kevin Miles once again. He was one of the FBI technical advisors for the film. According to Kevin, many of the investigative procedures were accurately portrayed, even the autopsy scene with Jennifer Garner's character. Kevin explained the ERT collects evidence from wherever they find it, even if that means removing shrapnel embedded in the bodies of victims, alive or deceased.

I enjoyed the film, until the over-the-top gun battle in the streets of Riyadh at the conclusion. That part was movie make-believe to the extreme. In reality, Kevin explained that FBI investigators and ERT members were forbidden to leave the Khobar Towers compound. Can you imagine foreign law enforcement officers shooting up a neighborhood in the United States and then returning to their home country the next day without reprisal?

My rating for *The Kingdom*: I kept my shoes on my feet, but during the film, I loosened the laces just in case.

#19

BAD GUYS PLOT REVENGE AGAINST THE FBI AGENTS WHO PUT THEM BEHIND BARS

Retaliation

A frequent storyline for books, TV shows, and movies is a bad guy setting up an elaborate scheme to play mind games with and exact revenge upon the agent who was responsible for sending them to prison. The FBI is very cautious about protecting its agents from harm, but threats are rare. Agents receive immediate transfers to safety if a credible threat is made against them or their loved ones.

It may surprise you to learn that in many circumstances, the subjects of FBI cases will maintain cordial contact with case agents during and after serving time in prison. These "bad guys" often call agents to let them know the name and location of the federal penitentiary where they're assigned and continue to keep in touch for many years following their release. During several of my *FBI Retired Case File Review* interviews, agents spoke about their friendships with former subjects and informants. I interviewed a former subject turned cooperating witness in episode 044, "Karl LNU - Cooperating Witness, Telemarketing Fraud," during which we spoke about our continued association. We have since conducted a well-received presentation together at a local university on how not to get scammed.

Placing an FBI agent in harm's way is one of the conventions of the thriller genre. The hero at the mercy of the villain is an obligatory scene and one of the highlights of crime novels and films, so I doubt if the revenge cliché will ever or should ever die. But at least now you know that because agents often use respect and empathy (as explained in the Chapter #9) in their interview techniques, in most cases, subjects understand that agents are just doing their job.

Witness intimidation is another story. Whether they be subtle messages warning against "snitching" or overt threats to discourage cooperation with the FBI, witness intimidation threatens the integrity of our criminal justice system. The FBI and law enforcement agencies in general rely and depend on the cooperation and testimony of witnesses. As is the case when an agent is threatened, witnesses may be informally relocated by the FBI or placed officially in the witness security protection (WITSEC) program.

Garland Schweickhardt, in episode 158, "FBI Hollywood Sting, The Last Shot," explained why he was never concerned for his safety when he was investigating the Boston mob:

Garland Schweickhardt (GS): And even after it was over, I ran into Salemme (the defendant in his case) when we were doing the preliminary hearings for the trial, and he attended those before he was dropped from the case because he got sick. I ran into him in the elevator. He just said, "Hi, how you doing?" He didn't act threatening to me. Even though my name became known during the trial, I was never worried they would take any action against me because I was FBI. They weren't going to do anything to me. Now, with Frankie and Hillary, they would have killed them. When they thought maybe I might be a cop, Frank Salemme Sr. had told Hillary, "If you're bringing my son into something, we're gonna kill you. We'll kill you. This better be legit. It better not be anything that gets him into trouble."

Hillary went into the witness protection program, and for a number of years, I stayed in contact with Hillary or Hillary would call me because they still had the FBI number. I asked him how he was doing, but I haven't talked to him in several years now.

Jerri Williams: Why do you think he wanted to keep that connection with you?

GS: We got along. In preparation for the trial, the trial lasted six weeks, and we were back there in Boston together during the trial and also during all the preparation for the preliminary hearings and so forth. We got along very well. And the case agent, Bill Fleming, he got along with him too.

FBI Film and Fiction Review

The Last Shot

In the 2004 star-studded comedy *The Last Shot*, actor Alec Baldwin played the role of real-life retired agent Garland Schweickhardt who sold Hollywood the rights to his life story, including his role in the investigation code-named Dramex for "Drama Expose," where he posed as an investment consultant for wealthy individuals who wanted to produce a non-union film. In the movie, the FBI plans to target a violent Boston mobster played by actor Tony Shalhoub. At the beginning of the movie, bad guys chop off Baldwin's character's finger. You'll be relieved to learn that the scene was creative license at play and the real Schweickhardt still has all of his digits. Matthew Broderick starred as the screenwriter/director unaware that the producer was really an FBI undercover agent. Actress Calista Flockhart played his girlfriend.

The Last Shot was a comedy and, consequently, purposely took the action over-the-top. It was, therefore, surprising to see so many scenes somewhat accurately depicting the critical-parent-like behavior of Bureau management and other issues that come up when conducting an undercover operation.

My rating for *The Last Shot*: I kept my shoes on my feet, but during the movie, I loosened the laces just in case.

#20 FBI AGENTS ARE PERFECT AND NEVER GET IN TROUBLE

Public Criticism

The most powerful weapon the FBI possesses is the agency's decades-long, earned reputation for integrity. For the most part, the Bureau leaves bad behavior to the Secret Service (just joking). Unfortunately, some agents have made serious mistakes and boneheaded transgressions, and have violated the understanding that the behavior of every FBI employee is a direct reflection on the Bureau's core values. It's expected that everything an FBI agent says and does will project a positive image and mirror the viewpoint of the "front office." That's because agents take that whole "fidelity, bravery, and integrity" stuff very seriously. Translated to real-life situations those words connote loyalty, confidence, and well…integrity.

Notwithstanding the misconduct of a few bad apples, there is a saying in the FBI: "Don't embarrass the Bureau." And there is also the belief that agents must strive to uphold the proud reputation of the FBI established during more than 110 years of service. This institutional reputation is what allows an agent to knock on a door, make a phone call, or walk into an interview room and receive instant credibility.

Not wanting to shy away from disconcerting moments in FBI history, I have conducted podcast case reviews recounting the investigation and convictions of several Bureau "bad boys": Robert Hanssen, who sold secrets to the former Soviet Union and KGB; Mark Putnam, who murdered his FBI informant and lover; and Ken Withers, who stole $200 million of Pakistani heroin from the Philadelphia Office's evidence room. I included these investigations because I believe that it is important to emphasize that they are anomalies to FBI agent behavior.

The FBI selects future employees through stringent hiring standards. The rigorous recruiting, background, and selection process for special agents helps the FBI weed out potential problems, or at least keep them to a minimum. The FBI's internal affairs department is called the Office of Professional Responsibility (OPR). When I was an active employee, OPR would issue a quarterly report of bad behavior and the punishment dealt out to the employee as a warning to all. By the way, the fastest way an agent can earn a letter of censure and a suspension (known as "time on the beach") is by misuse of a Bureau vehicle. Oh, the stories I could tell about "bu-car" infractions. New agents are warned never to do anything untoward in, on or near a Bureau car, because even if the conduct isn't a fireable offense, management can always hang an agent with the misuse of Bureau car violation.

Now, some may want me to add the conduct of certain FBI leaders during the 2016 presidential election to the above list of Bureau bad boys. However, it is my opinion that, although ultimately damaging to the non-political reputation of the FBI, the actions of these leaders— whether made with integrity and without bias or not —have nothing to do with the work of the average agent in the field. At the time of publication of *FBI Myths and Misconception: A Manual for Armchair Detectives*, the jury of public opinion is still in deliberation. History will determine the final verdict regarding the intentions and motivations of the FBI leaders in question, as has been the case at other times in the past when the FBI has come under scrutiny. The list includes former director J. Edgar Hoover's investigative mandates in relation to the Reverend Martin Luther King Jr. and the civil rights movement, the Watergate investigation that ultimately led to the resignation of President Richard Nixon, and the FBI's involvement in the deadly aftermath of militia standoffs, such as Waco.

Nevertheless, the FBI will continue to serve the people of the United States and the retired agent case reviews of the hundreds of cases of courage and sacrifice highlighted within these pages and the *FBI Retired Case File Review* podcast will continue to speak for the commitment to justice held by current and former special agents of the FBI.

FBI Film and Fiction Review

Breach

The 2007 American spy drama *Breach* covers the real-life investigation of Robert Hanssen, the FBI agent charged and convicted of spying for and selling secrets for more than twenty years to the former Soviet Union and KGB. Based on a series of compromised double agents, the FBI was aware that there was a mole among them, and Hanssen became the number-one suspect. The movie follows the assignment given to FBI surveillance group specialist Eric O'Neill to garner Hanssen's trust. O'Neill ultimately was able to obtain information from Hanssen's PalmPilot that would enable the agents to capture Hanssen in the act of clearing a drop. Eric O'Neill was played by actor Ryan Phillippe and Chris Cooper starred as Robert Hanssen. The movie showed the FBI's determination to make sure Hanssen suffered the consequences of his betrayal.

My rating for *Breach*: I kept my shoes on my feet, but during the movie, I loosened the laces just in case.

In episode 031, "FBI Betrayal, Robert Hanssen," Retired Agent Mike Rochford discussed the movie *Breach* and how, for a couple of months before Robert Hanssen was arrested, FBI support employee Eric O'Neill monitored Hanssen's office activities:

Mike Rochford (MR): O'Neill was able to get ahold of his PalmPilot, which gave us the date of his next planned drop for the KGB or the SVR.

Jerri Williams: In the movie, that was one of the suspenseful and exciting parts. What position did O'Neill have in the FBI? From my understanding of the movie, he was not an agent.

MR: No he wasn't. He was SSG surveillance. What we wanted to do was get somebody who was non-threatening and who would be able to see him every day. Even though Rich Garcia was his supervisor, Rich had to run a whole division. He didn't have time to be in touch with Hanssen every day. So we wanted to get somebody who was working in his office on a daily basis and who could report to another agent at the end of the day what was going on. That's largely what the movie *Breach* is based on—O'Neill's undercover interactions with Bob. The movie attributes a lot of things to Mr. O'Neill that probably were done by agents, but that's the movies.

———

One of the most perilous ways an agent can be compromised is in an inappropriate relationship with a source. Agents are mandated to have a second agent attend meetings and to witness payments. Even when developing a close bond is acceptable, clear limits must be established. Ignoring and crossing boundaries between agents and informants have been the downfall of many.

FBI Film and Fiction Review

Above Suspicion

Above Suspicion is the true-crime book, published in 1993, that covers the tragic outcome of the forbidden relationship between FBI agent Mark Putnam and his pregnant informant Susan Smith. It was a book by author Joe Sharkey, and there's a yet-to-be-released movie by the same name, starring actors Emilia Clarke and Jack Huston. Putnam was a fairly new agent who, after graduating from the FBI Academy in 1987, was assigned to a two-person resident agency in Pikesville, Kentucky, high in Appalachian coal country, where he received minimal training and supervision. The satellite office was several hours away from Louisville, the main field office. Putnam opened Susan Smith as a source supplying information about drug deals.

They began a torrid affair that he soon regretted and hoped would end after he was transferred to another office. However, when Susan Smith learned she was pregnant, she threatened to tell Putnam's wife and his FBI superiors. In a moment of panic, he strangled her and tossed her body into a ravine. Initially, he was above suspicion due to his position and reputation. The book and movie recount the shocking conclusion of the FBI's investigation into the disappearance and suspected murder of Smith and how the scandal and murder affected the small mining community.

I didn't read the book *Above Suspicion* and the film is not out yet, so I'm unable to rate either. However, retired agent Jim Huggins provided his thoughts.

In episode 066, "Mark Putnam, FBI Informant Murderer," retired agent Jim Huggins talked about his experience as a technical adviser during the filming of the yet-to-be released movie, *Above Suspicion*:

Jerri Williams (JW): How did you feel about the film and all the other films and books that were written about this case?

Jim Huggins (JH): I think there were a couple TV shows I saw which were not accurate at all. One of the books that came out earlier was way off base. They were trying to give the theme that this was a premeditated murder, and the FBI was trying to cover it up and protect their own agent, which is totally bogus. I was really interested in becoming involved in this movie with the great director they had and the producers who were all interested in telling the true story. They gave me complete leeway in making suggestions and changes to the script. I think, in the end, they got it exactly right. I think it's going to be an outstanding movie, although it's a very sad case for everybody concerned. It will show how it all happened and how the FBI conducted the investigation, which ultimately led to Mark's confession and later conviction.

They've got some dramatic scenes in there that didn't happen, but there's nothing to deviate from the facts of the case. It's just action shots, where shots are fired here and there when they're chasing a bank robber. That kind of stuff.

JW: They always throw that stuff in.

JH: I told Philip Noyce, the director, "Philip, you know how you can't shoot a guy running like that in the back." He said, "Well, how would you do it?" I got him to change it around a little bit so it would make half sense. But I said, "No one ever fired a shot." He said, "But you've got to have some action, mate." He's an Australian guy. "You got to have some action, or people won't sit in the movie for two hours."

But there's just little things like that. Nothing that detracted from the facts. The movie is about two people who came together with their own ambitions and how it all just fell apart.

———

There are no acceptable reasons for an FBI agent to leak information to journalists or the public. Any FBI employee who believes that an investigation is being improperly handled and wishes to report possible illegal actions or mismanagement has more appropriate avenues to consider under the Whistleblower Protection Program.

Retired agent Angelo Lano, in episode 063, "FBI Watergate Investigation," spoke about being suspected of being Deep Throat and what he thought when Mark Felt admitted years later to leaking information to the Washington Post:

Jerri Williams (JW): Well, let's talk about the leaks too. Of course, there is Deep Throat. Somebody is leaking information to *Washington Post* reporters; you mentioned them yourself, Woodward and Bernstein. You were falsely accused of possibly being Deep Throat.

Angelo Lano (AL): I think some professor out at...I can't remember the name of the university. I think it was University of Chicago or something like that.

They had pursued a review of the entire case, and they came up with a couple of suspects, and I was named as one of them.

JW: What do you think about that?

AL: I thought it was lousy. It wasn't me.

JW: So when you found out that it was an FBI agent, the second in command, Mark Felt…?

AL: He actually was one of several that we later determined from headquarters had been speaking to people in the press. I mean there were leaks to *TIME Magazine*; there were leaks to the *New York Times*, the *Los Angeles Times*. Mark Felt was responsible for a great deal of it, I'm sure. But there were instances where there was other information passed, and we felt it was coming from somewhere else in the department.

JW: And when you say the department, the Justice Department or the FBI?

AL: The FBI.

JW: Wow.

AL: But it definitely wasn't any street agent because we work with grand juries. We work criminal cases most of our life. Why would we go out and jeopardize our own case? Why would we tell the public what we're investigating? Just like what's going on today. Why would you tell anybody what you're doing? Grand jury is supposed to be secret until the end results come out.

JW: Years later, when it was determined that it was Mark Felt, what did you think about that?

AL: I wasn't too shocked. I always felt that it was somebody higher up in the Bureau, somebody with access just like we all had. And, of course, he was just one person who was upset over the fact that some outsider was going to be appointed director and not him.

———

FBI agents hold their leaders to a high standard and expect their decisions and actions to be based on sound judgement and good intentions.

FBI Film and Fiction Review

Mark Felt: The Man Who Brought Down the White House

This 2017 biographical political thriller takes a heroic point of view as it covers the story of the unveiling of the mysterious "Deep Throat," most likely because the movie was based on the 2006 autobiography of FBI agent Mark Felt, played in the movie by actor Liam Neeson. In 1972, someone working under the name "Deep Throat" was providing unauthorized information to *Washington Post* reporters Bob Woodward and Carl Bernstein. Felt confessed just before he died that he was the individual who helped the journalists unravel the Watergate scandal, only steps behind FBI investigators. At the time of the leaks, the entire country could only speculate about the identity of the anonymous source with an inside scoop on the investigation. The film follows Felt's clandestine meetings with the journalists and attempts to lay out his reasons for doing so. The scandal ultimately led to the resignation of President Richard Nixon. Diane Lane and Tony Goldwyn also star in the film. Real-life FBI agent Angelo Lano was portrayed by Ike Barinholtz in this true-crime drama.

My rating for *Mark Felt: The Man Who Brought Down the White House*: I kept my shoes on my feet, but during the movie, I loosened the laces just in case.

AFTERWORD

Recognition of Creative Compromise

As stated at the introduction of *FBI Myths and Misconceptions: A Manual for Armchair Detectives*, when writers are crafting their books and scripts, the most important thing is the story. As I've conducted my own examination into the FBI clichés that have developed in film and fiction, I realized that there is a precarious relationship between reality and the creative process. The writer's job is to pull the reader or viewer into the story and eliminate distractions that may shatter those connections, even if it means cutting facts and creating alternative ones. This is the case even when the story is true. That's why the words "based on a true story" or "based on real events" are sometimes noted on the cover of a book or movie poster.

The following language was used in an option agreement for the rights to an agent's life story: "It is Producer's intention to portray optioned materials as factually as possible with the understanding that Producer has the right to make changes. No approval rights are granted whatsoever in connection with any scripts created or motion pictures produced hereunder, which rights shall be held solely and exclusively by Producer and shall include, without limitation, control over all dramatic elements of said scripts and motion pictures and or television series."

Based on the contract, the agent will have no control in whether or not he or the FBI is accurately portrayed in the series.

When FBI agents read or watch these modified true tales, it often frustrates them. I recently read an agent's harsh condemnation of a miniseries regarding a major FBI investigation. It has been acknowledged that the TV show took artistic license to make one of the agents appear to have a bigger role in the actual case than he did. The argument was that, in the series, the agents who actually lead the task force weren't acknowledged. However, those decisions to create one composite character were made by the show's writers and producers. FBI agents who have sold the rights to their life stories to Hollywood, quickly learn that they no longer have control over how their stories are told. However, even with fictionalized cop shows, when the FBI is shown doing things that would never happen in real life, the dramas are a turn off for those in law enforcement who might be watching.

However, such creative compromises are made in the entertainment world every day. Books and films succeed or fail based on their ability to capture and engage an audience. These creative compromises regarding how the FBI really works are used to move the story at a certain pace, create conflict, and provide entertainment—that's the key. Hopefully, the writer will also try to keep the story as true to life as possible and honor the agents who do the job.

So, in conducting my research and pulling together these top twenty clichés and misconceptions about the FBI in books, TV, and movies, I must also consider that perhaps readers and viewers are more concerned with being entertained than being educated.

As a writer of crime fiction myself, I have to be willing to go beyond the facts, to use creative license, to add a little juice to pump up routine FBI tasks. My crime novels pull from my personal experiences. After years of writing just-the-facts FD-302s, I had to allow myself to reimagine real-life scenarios and know that was okay. My Philadelphia corruption squad series, featuring Special Agent Kari Wheeler, is a police procedural with a redemption theme inspired by actual FBI cases—but with the boring parts of working a case left out. Because I'm writing in a fictionalized setting, I'm able to expand the stories and take my characters where I believe my readers want the story to go. Her painful past and flaws have her doing things that would get real FBI agents into serious trouble. It should be noted that although Special Agent Kari Wheeler may at first glance seem familiar, my husband wants me to make sure readers know she is not me. Ha-ha.

FBI Case File Review Podcast

If you're a loyal listener and longtime subscriber: Thanks for listening. If you are not already listening to *FBI Retired Case File Review*, why not?

I love reading crime fiction, especially police procedurals where the story follows the investigators as they attempt to solve a crime. I figured people who liked to read stories about the FBI, would also like to listen to them, so I decided to produce a podcast where I would interview retired FBI agents about their cases and careers and review crime fiction—I thought it was a good niche idea. True crime is an exploding genre, and there were already many popular true crime podcasts, but none that exclusively featured FBI agents and the crime fiction, true crime books and memoirs they had written. I also wanted to discuss what books, TV, and movies often got wrong about the FBI. But would I be able to attract an audience for the show? I posted my first episode to iTunes, now known as Apple Podcast, on January 22, 2016 and *FBI Retired Case File Review* now has a robust domestic and international following.

But soon things got serious. In the summer of 2016, then FBI Director James Comey held an unprecedented news conference where he announced a prosecutive decision not to recommend criminal charges against Democratic presidential candidate Hillary Clinton. Such announcements are usually made through the Department of Justice by the attorney general or a United States attorney. The remarks he made catapulted the FBI into the volatile political climate. Other issues have occurred that continue to keep the FBI in partisan news stories.

My FBI true crime and history podcast that began as a marketing tool to introduce myself to potential readers of my crime fiction morphed into what is today, my personal mission to show the public who the FBI is and what the FBI does, and assure them of the integrity and independence of the Bureau. I believe it's essential for the public to have a transparent view of the FBI.

I find my retired agent guests by looking for interesting cases and agent profiles featured in *The Grapevine*, the monthly publication of the Society of Former Special Agents of the FBI, and from following the much-welcomed suggestions received from listeners. I then use my investigative skills to locate the case agents. I also search the internet for articles about retired agents and I, of course, reach out to my FBI friends and former coworkers and ask them (beg them) to share their fascinating stories and insights. I'm honored to share these FBI stories with the public. Podcasting makes me happy.

I would be disingenuous, if I didn't add that I initially developed my podcast to distinguish my work and establish my authority and expertise in the crime fiction field. I truly appreciate the fact that the success of *FBI Retired Case File Review* has allowed me to reach potential readers and build a community of supportive fans.

One of the reasons I'm especially proud of these interviews is that, in the Bureau, when they promote FBI successes, they usually leave out the names of the investigators in the press release. In conducting these investigations, many agents have dedicated their lives, sacrificed their marriages, and spent time away from their kids. To talk about a case without acknowledging the sacrifices made by those FBI agents and employees who work those cases is not good. The public needs to know that the FBI is made up of people. They need to learn who the FBI is and what the FBI does by hearing directly from those involved, not just from reading a sanitized narrative announced by the head of the office. Based on current times, this type of transparent look at the FBI is needed more than ever, don't you think?

Each of the *FBI Retired Case File Review* episodes can serve as the inspiration for a crime novel, movie, or TV show. More than two-hundred violations of federal laws are under the FBI's jurisdiction. Even agents and law enforcement personnel with two or three decades in the trenches express how much they enjoy listening to the fascinating case reviews. The true stories allow them to experience what it's like to hunt down a spy during a counterintelligence espionage case or comb through a file cabinet of incriminating documents in a white-collar crime corruption investigation. This fact helps me appreciate how much writers and readers must also be starved for an opportunity to practically eavesdrop on the FBI, to be a fly on the wall to history. I'm excited by the future story concepts these true crime and history reviews might prompt.

I label *FBI Retired Case File Review* the "diet" or "lite" version of true crime. Most true crime podcasts feature mass quantities of blood, gore, murder, and mayhem. However, in most FBI investigations, there's not a lot of bloody bedlam, but there is intrigue and suspense. Perhaps my brand of true crime, with a large heaping of history, offers even more captivating ideas and premises for authors to explore.

At the time of the publication of *FBI Myths and Misconceptions: A Manual for Armchair Detectives,* I have interviewed nearly two-hundred retired agents about some of the Bureau's biggest historically significant cases, as well as many fascinating but not-as-well-known investigations. Among the many agents I've had the pleasure to speak with are the case agents of the Miami Shootout, Unabomber, Bernie Madoff, Polly Klaas, Robert Hanssen, Watergate, Jeffrey Dahmer, and Oklahoma City bombing investigations.

FBI Retired Case File Review is available on my website, jerriwilliams.com, Apple Podcast, Google Podcast, Spotify, and other popular podcast apps, as well as YouTube. The show's healthy growth comes from good old fashion word-of-mouth promotion.

FBI Reading Resource

Of course, another way to make sure you're getting accurate information about the FBI and being entertained at the same time is to read books about the FBI written by FBI agents. I'm always excited to speak to the other retired agents also writing books. More of us are becoming authors, whether writing fiction or nonfiction inspired by our cases. I've made it easy for you to find them by curating a colorful exclusive listing of crime fiction, thrillers, true crime, and memoirs by the retired agents featured on the *FBI Retired Case File Review* podcast. I call my book list the FBI Reading Resource, and it's available to members of my Reader Team. When you join my Reader Team, in addition to the FBI Reading Resource, I'll also send the FBI Reality Checklist, a printable PDF of the twenty clichés and misconceptions featured in *FBI Myths and Misconceptions: A Manual for Armchair Detectives* and my monthly email digest, where I make it easy for you to keep up-to-date on the FBI in books, TV, and movies. You can join my Reader Team when you visit my website **jerriwilliams.com.** There's also a direct link in the back of this book.

Bypass the Entertainment and News Media

My initial observation at the beginning of *FBI Myths and Misconceptions: A Manual for Armchair Detectives* was that what most people know about the FBI comes from popular culture, books, TV, and movies, as well as the news. If you're curious about the FBI but have no plans to apply, write a book, or produce a TV show or movie, you still don't have to rely on information created by individuals and organizations with no connection to the Bureau. There are several additional resources available to the average person wanting to learn more about the FBI.

Ask An Agent

People assume that what agents do is a secret, that it's all covert. But that's not true. Yes, there may be agents who are assigned to counterintelligence or counterterrorism cases that will never be in the public domain. However, for the most part, an FBI agent can discuss any FBI investigation that has been fully adjudicated and is in the public domain. Just turn on your TV—there are entire true crime TV networks and cable news outlets featuring sound bites from retired agents. So if you ever meet an FBI agent, ask your questions. Most will be happy to provide answers.

FBI.gov Website

To learn about the FBI directly from the FBI, you can visit and browse FBI.gov. I find it easier to locate information by using Google search, instead of the FBI website search bar, which doesn't seem to distinguish key word results for focused articles and simple mentions. In addition to the information offered on the FBI website, details about employment and the wide variety of jobs available in the FBI can be found on the FBIJobs.gov website.

Citizens Academy

Did you know that FBI field offices offer an interactive course providing an inside view of how the FBI operates to local community leaders? The classes are held for six to eight weeks, usually in the evening. The purpose of the Citizen's Academy is to liaison with business, religious, civic, and non-profit organizations and develop a transparent partnership between them and the local FBI division that serves the community. Attendees are educated about the different violations investigated by the FBI, learn how to process a crime scene, train with firearms, some may even tour FBI Headquarters and the FBI Academy. Participants must apply for consideration and are selected by the special agent in charge of the local FBI field office. To learn more, contact the FBI field office closest to where you live.

Investigative Publicity and Public Affairs Unit

I believe the major clichés about the FBI are addressed and resolved in *FBI Myths and Misconceptions: A Manual for Armchair Detectives*. However, writers and producers who have additional questions about who the FBI is and what the FBI does may want to contact the FBI's Investigative Publicity and Public Affairs Unit (IPPAU), located at FBI headquarters. As you may recall from the introduction, during the last five years of my FBI career, I served as the media representative and spokesperson for the Philadelphia Division. During this time, I worked directly with the FBI Headquarters public affairs staff on a regular basis.

The agents and public affairs specialists in the unit respond to inquiries from the news media, but they are also actively handling questions posed by authors, writers, and producers who seek information to assist them in creating accurate portrayals of the FBI and its special agents. The IPPAU's mission is identical to mine—to show the public who the FBI is and what the FBI does. I accomplish these tasks through my books, my blog, and my podcast. The IPPAU does it by working with the news and entertainment media. Their goal goes beyond illuminating "the FBI brand." They are also striving to build and maintain the American people's trust in the Bureau, with the awareness that the public's cooperation will assist the FBI with its operational mission.

Working with the news and entertainment media, doesn't mean that news articles, books, or TV shows, and movies will always reflect the FBI in a positive light or provide a flattering portrayal of the work that agents do. But the Investigative Publicity and Public Affairs Unit liaison with reporters, producers, authors, writers, and filmmakers helps make sure the truth is out there. It's up to them to determine when and how to use the information provided.

Based on its limited staff and resources, the IPPAU cannot ensure cooperation with every project. However, as determined on a case-by-case basis, they may be able to provide information on FBI policies and procedures, provide access to FBI facilities and personnel for filming and interviews, fact-check articles, manuscripts and screenplays, and provide guidance on FBI history and current operations.

From the FBI Website

"Frequently Ask Questions"
How can screenwriters, authors, and producers seeking authenticity work with the FBI?

If you are a writer, author, or producer who wants to feature the FBI, we may be able to work with you to create an accurate portrayal of the Bureau. We've been doing it since the 1930s. Specifically, the Investigative Publicity and Public Affairs Unit (IPPAU), in our Office of Public Affairs is a small staff that spends a portion of its time working with domestic and international screenwriters, producers, authors, and other industry personnel associated with TV programs, documentaries, made-for-TV movies, books, and motion pictures. In addition, the unit is the same one that manages national and international publicity for wanted fugitives (including the Ten Most Wanted Fugitives), Most Wanted Terrorists, and missing children, and it also coordinates other proactive initiatives.

(https://www.fbi.gov/about/faqs/how-can-screenwriters-authors-and-producers-seeking-authenticity-work-with-the-fbi)

————

It has been an honor and pleasure to use my twenty-six years of service in the FBI and my unique experiences interviewing nearly two-hundred retired agents to write *FBI Myths and Misconceptions: A Manual for Armchair Detectives*. By debunking twenty of the most common clichés and misconceptions, I hope I've been able to show you who the FBI is and what the FBI does.

Thank you!

I hope you enjoyed *FBI Myths and Misconceptions: A Manual for Armchair Detectives.*

Please take a moment to write a short review and post it on the online retailer where you purchased the book. Reviews help readers find good books.

Visit: jerriwilliams.com

Join my Reader Team here (http://eepurl.com/ dAIh59) to receive the FBI Reading Resource— books about the FBI written by FBI agents; the printable FBI Reality Checklist; updates on the FBI in books, TV, and movies; and more via my monthly email digest!

ABOUT THE AUTHOR

Jerri Williams, a retired FBI special agent, jokes that she writes crime fiction in an attempt to relive her glory days. After twenty-six years with the Bureau specializing in major economic fraud and corruption investigations,  she calls on her professional encounters with scams and schemers to write books inspired by real FBI cases. Jerri is also the host and producer of *FBI Retired Case File Review*, a true crime podcast. She resides with her husband in South Jersey, just across the river from Philadelphia. You can find out more about Jerri at www.jerriwilliams.com. You can also connect with her on Twitter and Instagram @jerriwilliams1 or Facebook at Jerri Williams Author.

Also check out Jerri's FBI crime series featuring FBI Agent Kari Wheeler assigned to a Philadelphia corruption squad. Available as ebooks, paperbacks, and audiobooks:

Pay To Play

Greedy Givers

Spoiled Sport (2020)

ACKNOWLEDGMENTS

Many people have played important roles from the first draft to the publication of *FBI Myths and Misconceptions: A Manual for Armchair Detectives*. Special thanks to the many professionals who guided me on the development and design of the book. I'm also grateful for my friend and developmental editor Sue Olsen; my super squad of beta readers, Judy Tyler, Lisa Williams, and Janine Williams; and the supportive members of my advance reader team.

I also express love and gratitude to my husband, Keith Wert, for his patience as I sequester myself in my home office for hours at a time to get the words down on paper.

FBI Myths and Misconceptions: A Manual for Armchair Detectives was inspired by my love of writing and reading crime novels and my true crime and history podcast *FBI Retired Case File Review*. I dedicate this book to the readers and listeners interested in learning who the FBI is and what the FBI does.

Thank you all for your support!

Jerri

INDEX